FROM
Hollywood
TO
Heaven

R O B I N   H A R F O U C H E

FROM

Hollywood

TO

Heaven

FOREWORD BY
CHARLENE TILTON

Power House Publishing

Pensacola, Florida

From Hollywood to Heaven
Published by:
Power House Publishing
2411 Executive Plaza Rd.
Pensacola, FL 32504
ISBN 0-9634451-8-9

Cover design by:
DB & Associates Design Group, Inc.
dba Double Blessing Productions
P.O. Box 52756, Tulsa, Oklahoma 74152
www.doubleblessing.com
Cover illustration is protected by the 1976
United States Copyright Act.

Interior design and production by:
Cathleen L. Kwas / CLicK Services
Lake Mary, Florida 32746

Printed in the United States of America

Dedication

This book is dedicated to my husband, Christian, the first person who made me realize I could trust again.

Contents

Foreword

*F*rom the time I first met Robin about twenty years ago, our outings together always proved to be quite an adventure. Two Hollywood starlets, and blonde nonetheless, we were a staple of Hollywood's "Who's Who" party scene, and couldn't buy a dull moment if we tried.

Robin was always, and still is, the type of person that no matter what she undertakes she gives it all she has, quickly moving to the top. This was particularly evident in her dance career. I mean, really, who begins a professional dance career at the age of 18 after only having begun to train at 18!? In the Biz, that's unheard of and yet, that's just what Robin did! An award winning choreographer, Robin was not only my dance instructor but she also coached such stars as Kirk Douglas and Billy Crystal for Broadway shows. In addition, her acting had taken off, being repped by one of the top agencies in the world, which, as any actor knows is not a small accomplishment.

The persistent longing in her heart for the meaning and purpose of her life, however, overshadowed all of this. As a result, her quest took her into deep realms of the supernatural. After years of searching, Robin found the answer she so desperately craved.

I listen and watch in amazement as she shares her story, touching hearts like no other, and I realize that Robin has the same darling personality she's always had. She's still Robin...only better. And I'm thrilled to call her my friend.

— Charlene Tilton
Actress

Introduction

The reach of the Spirit is touching and changing people from every walk of life and in every way imaginable. Never before has the universal family encountered such a time of global spiritual awakening.

During her quest to find the peace she desperately needed, Robin met an unexpected turn of events that left her the recipient of a global mission. As you join Robin in *From Hollywood to Heaven* (her true story), fasten your seat belt for the most exhilarating journey of your life.

— Christian Harfouche

Chapter 1

The Woman in the Woods

The log cabin was damp and cold. Wrapping a threadbare quilt around my shoulders, I inched to the edge of the bed, dropped lightly onto the dirt floor, and padded over to the window on bare feet. It was twilight, and the rising moon spilled silver streaks into the darkness of the cabin. If I strained my eyes I could make out the stark furnishings of the room: two roughly hewn chairs, a table, and the creaky iron bed I had just left. A handmade rock fireplace against the far wall sat frozen with disuse. Its stones gleamed eerily pale in the faint light, giving it more the appearance of an igloo than a place intended for warmth.

How did I get here? I wondered, turning again toward the open window. A thick wood surrounded the cabin, its leafless trees making ominous shapes in the deepening dark. I shivered. This was no place of comfort. A sense of foreboding clutched at my chest.

Suddenly, I saw a woman on horseback galloping toward me down a narrow path cut through the woods. I stood transfixed, unable to do anything but watch and wait.

The woman was wearing a long, dark blue dress, very unlike the dresses my mother always wore. On her feet were shiny black riding boots. A dark, hooded cloak flapped wildly as she drew nearer on her brilliant white steed, her piercing eyes glaring at me. She drew the horse up to a walk, never averting her eyes from mine. They were the coldest steel-blue eyes I had ever seen. They seemed to beckon me against my will.

"What do you want?" I screamed, my voice shrill with terror. "What do you want with me?"

Something magnetic pulled me toward her, and unseen hands pushed me from behind toward the door, which now swung open by itself.

"No!" I screamed, wrestling with a creature I could not see. "Let me go!"

I turned and struck it, and it shrank back in the shadows.

A muffled thump came from outside the cabin. I wheeled in time to see the woman, dismounted, heading straight for me. The same unseen hands gripped my arms and propelled me toward the horrible woman in blue.

"No! No! No!" I cried, my strength waning.

My eyes flew open. No woman. No hands. Only darkness and the thumping of my own heart. A chilly California breeze played with the crisp yellow curtains that framed my bedroom window. Panting and soaked with sweat, I groped around the bedcovers for familiar objects. Yes. There was Teddy. There was my Chatty Cathy doll. I continued groping until my fingers closed around something cold and metallic. It was the crucifix Grandma had brought back from her trip to the Vatican, and my constant nighttime companion.

Still trembling with fright, I murmured into the darkness, "Our Father, which art in heaven, hallowed be Thy name...." I couldn't remember where I had learned the words—certainly not in church, for my family never went—but they always comforted me. Somewhere between darkness and dawn a gentle sleep enfolded me in safety.

"Wake up, creep," a loud voice said, jarring my ears. It was my sister, Debbie. Only two years older than me, she was the tough one in the family. Even at seven she could snarl at the neighborhood tormentors, the dozen or so boys who terrorized us smaller kids, and send them yelping for home. I was not like Debbie. Preferring ruffled pinafores to her blue jeans and leather jacket, I was the natural target for the local bullies.

"Get out of bed, lazy head," she singsonged.

"Mom said rise and shine."

"I'm up, I'm up," I said, rubbing the sleep from my eyes. "What time is it? I thought it was Saturday."

"Nope. Friday," came the retort. "Gotta get ready for school, Sleeping Beauty." Debbie sauntered out of the room, already dressed and ready for breakfast.

It was May 1962, and only two weeks of kindergarten stood between me and the glorious promise of summer vacation. It had been a bad year. Mom worried because I hadn't settled in at school like the other kids. Always the sensitive one, I got teased regularly; sometimes I was hit. I drew into myself and became even quieter. Now first grade loomed in the not-too-distant future as a dreaded prison term.

"Who cares?" I said out loud, kicking the covers into a ball. Deep inside I knew I did care, but I stuffed the fear down into a tiny little hole in my heart.

After pulling on the clothes Mom had laid out for me, I stumbled down the hall to the bathroom. The little girl in the mirror gazed back at me with big, greenish-brown eyes. Hazel eyes, Dad called them. I splashed cold water on my face then tiptoed into my parents' bedroom.

"Mom," I began, hopping up onto the bed, "I keep having the same dream at night. It scares me."

My mother was standing at her vanity, her back to me. Dressed in a pistachio-green knit suit and stiletto heels, she looked lovelier than the movie star everyone said she resembled.

"What was the dream about, Robin?" she asked absently, taking this and that necklace from the jewelry knobs that lined the front of her dresser. I hesitated, waiting until she had settled on one particular necklace before pouring out my story. Mom grew quiet as I detailed the woman in blue who always came for me at night. When I finished, she still hadn't turned to face me. At last she turned around with a strange look on her face.

"Describe the lady to me again." I did, painting every detail vividly.

"That sounds exactly like my grandmother," she said, her voice trembling. "I remember when I was a little girl my grandmother used to scare me to death. I didn't want to be near her. I believe she was a witch."

I must have blanched pale as a ghost, because Mom quickly added, "But don't worry, honey. She's dead now."

When I finally made it to the breakfast table, Debbie was already munching her cereal, her attention riveted to the back of the Cornflakes box. My two brothers, Bobby and

Kevin, were slurping down the last soggy remnants of theirs, bowls tipped up and covering their faces. Bobby, age nine, was the oldest of us four kids. Kevin was a year younger than me and the only one not in real school. Mom dropped him off at a preschool on her way to work each morning.

"Robin, you'll just have to skip breakfast and grab a banana to eat on the bus," Mom said as she came into the room. "No, no, don't even sit down. The bus'll be here in five minutes." Grabbing her purse, she corralled the four of us out the door.

"I want you to take care of your sister, you hear me?" She called after Debbie, who was trotting toward the bus stop. "She's your own flesh and blood, for heaven's sake."

Turning to kiss my mother good-bye, I paused and looked at her perhaps a little too earnestly for a five-year-old.

"Robin, what is it?" she asked, smoothing a stray blond hair back into her neat French twist. "I've got to go to work, honey. Speak."

"Mama, will the scary lady come for me again tonight?" I bit my lower lip to stop it from quivering.

"There, there," she shushed, pulling my head to her. "It was just a nightmare, sweetie. Don't worry about it. Hurry, now, and catch up with your brother and sister."

I wanted to say more. I wanted to tell her how vividly real the dreams were, how terrified I was to go to bed at night. I wanted to tell her I sometimes saw things, creatures, that nobody else seemed to see. Instead I only nodded in silence and turned to make my way to the bus stop, head down.

The big yellow school bus rumbled to a stop, its brakes screeching. Clambering on board with the other children, I took the seat beside my sister.

"Pssst. Hey, Pollyanna!" I didn't have to turn my head to know who it was. The raspy voice belonged to none other than Dougie Doyle, the fiercest of the tormentors. I pushed my face against the bus window, ignoring the taunt, and gazed out at nothing in particular. Maybe he would leave me alone.

"I said *Pollyanna*. Cat got yer tongue?" This last jeer roused hoots of laughter from the big kids on the bus, including my sister. I kept silent.

"Looky here, Pollyanna," Dougie continued, "I'll let you squeak by this time, but you're mine after school, got that?"

A murmur of admiration went up, and Dougie finished the ride to school as king for the day. I hugged my lunchbox tight against my chest, blinking back tears. He would never see me cry.

Dougie was true to his word. That afternoon he and his gang stood outside our peach stucco house hurling taunts at my bedroom window. Mom and Dad were still at work, and the bullies knew it. It was open season at the Harry household.

"Fraidy-cat, fraidy-cat! Robin Harry's a fraidy-cat! Ha, ha, ha, ha, ha!" Dougie's vicious laughter reached my ears, despite the pillow I had pulled over my head. Debbie watched for my reaction with a mixture of curiosity and delight. My brothers were slouched in the den watching TV.

The taunts grew louder.

"Whatsa matter, crybaby, did we scare you? Boo-hoo-hoo, the baby's gonna stay inside and cry," Dougie mocked.

Something snapped inside me. Leaping out of bed, I strode down the hall straight for my parent's room. I knew what I had to do. I grabbed one of Dad's belts out of the closet and headed for the front door. The belt's thick leather strap and large, heavy buckle would do nicely.

I flung open the front door. There stood Dougie, eyes wide with surprise. He glanced at the belt in my hands, and for the first time I saw fear on his freckled face. Seeing it felt good. Not giving him time to think, I stomped right up to him and lashed at his head with all my might with the buckle end of the belt.

High-pitched screams pierced the quiet neighborhood street, and Dougie's cronies scattered for home. Only my victim lay there, curled up in a pitiful heap, a pool of bright red blood darkening the lawn.

The front door crashed open. Debbie and the boys bounded outside to see the gruesome sight.

Kevin took one look at Dougie, lying still on the grass, and screamed, "Robin's killed him! Robin's killed him! What are we gonna do?"

"Shut up," Debbie snapped, taking control.

"Bobby, go and call his mother. Kevin, you go get a wet cloth and some Band-Aids. You know where Mom keeps them." The boys nodded and ran to their errands. But I think we all realized Band-Aids wouldn't help this time.

I stood there gawking at what my hands had done. Had I really killed him? Stomach acids surged to my mouth. I ran back inside, slamming the front door so hard the porch light shattered.

"Hey, wait a minute," Debbie called, her voice dulled by the sound of tinkling shards of glass. "You did this, twerp. Come back here!" But it was too late. My feet were moving on their own now, and they carried me to the safety of my bedroom. Locking the door behind me, I crouched down in the corner beside my white canopy bed. Sobbing quietly, I awaited my fate.

Chapter 2

Life Changes

*L*oud rapping at the door jolted me out of sleep. At first I couldn't remember why I was curled up in the corner. "Robin! Open up, young lady," my father insisted. "You have a lot of explaining to do." Then I remembered. Dougie.

"Did you hear me? I said open up!" Dad's voice boomed.

Dreading the worst, I opened the door and saw my father's scowling face.

"You could've killed that kid!" he shouted, lifting his hand to slap me. The blow knocked me against the bed. "Just what am I going to tell his parents, that I've raised a maniac?" From somewhere Dad produced a paddle, and he spanked me again and again, never giving me a chance to explain my side of the story.

"But, Dad, he always hurts me," I sobbed, my voice muffled as I put my hands over my face. "I had to." My father paid no attention to my words. At last satisfied with his discipline, he stopped, heaving with exertion, and left the room. Almost as an afterthought he looked back at me and said, "Don't come out of this room until I say so." My bedroom became a prison. As the long minutes passed I pressed my ear to the door to gather tidbits of family conversation, all about the belting I had given Dougie Doyle. I learned in this secondhand fashion that Dougie would live after all. He had been taken to a hospital, where his head was stitched up and patched with a huge bandage. The phone rang continually. The neighbors wanted to know: was it true? Had little Robin actually given that bully whatfor? At first my mother's strained voice offered the explanations. But after about the third call, Dad took over, his voice terse and defensive.

Upon my return to the bus stop Monday morning, all the kids parted to let me pass through. My chest swelled with this new-found respect. Dougie was nowhere in sight. Rumor had it his mother was driving him to school.

Life resumed normalcy at the house, and before I knew it the remaining two weeks of kindergarten were over. I burst out of the school doors that last day and skipped all the way to the bright yellow bus, which sat waiting by the curb to take me to my freedom. Excited chatter filled the short ride home, each child exaggerating what he or she planned to do that summer.

What would I do? I wondered silently. Oh, well. It didn't matter. Just being out of school was enough. I smiled to myself.

That night after supper was cleared away, Mom and Dad took me aside. My father had become much gentler toward me since the horrible beating. He drew me up onto his lap in his favorite chair, while Mom took a seat across from us on the plaid sofa. She picked at little fuzz balls on her skirt, then glanced up, waiting for my father to begin.

"Bob, shall I tell her?" she said.

I looked up at him questioningly. He nodded at my mother, who took a deep breath and said, "Robin, your father and I know you've not been very happy this past year, what with school and those boys pestering you and all. We've been thinking it over and decided it would be good for you to stay at Grandma and Grandpa's for the summer. How would you like that, sweetheart?" I couldn't believe my ears. It was wonderful! Grandma and Grandpa lived on a prune ranch about forty-five minutes from our small, suburban town of Vallejo. Nestled in the head of Napa Valley, the ranch to me was like a scene out of a big, glossy picture book, or perhaps like the TV show "Big Valley" I always watched with my brothers.

"Do you mean it?" I squealed. "Can I really go?" Relieved at my reaction, Mom and Dad exchanged smiles and assured me that everything had already been prepared. My grandparents would come for me in four days.

A flurry of packing made the days pass quickly. I strutted around the house, flaunting to my jealous siblings that I, and not they, had been the chosen one. All of us loved the ranch. Every so often we drove the bumpy miles out to see Grandma and Grandpa, and we kids would spend the day romping in the hay, eating apples right off the tree, and playing hide-and-seek in the cool, shady barn.

At last the big day arrived. I watched from the window as Grandpa's green pickup truck turned in the driveway.

"Robin, they're here," Mom called.

I scampered down the hallway and threw myself into Grandma's arms.

"Well, hello there!" she said, rumpling my dirty-blond

hair. "Are you ready to go?"

"Uh-huh," I said, smiling shyly.

Grandpa stepped inside the house behind her. Before he could shout a greeting we all rushed at him, squealing with delight. Grandpa was everyone's favorite. After a short visit, Dad and Grandpa loaded my suitcases into the back of the truck. I hugged the family good-bye and jumped in the front seat between the two people I loved best in the world. Waving excitedly, I watched until the figures of my parents, brothers, and sister grew tiny. At last a bend in the road blotted them from sight. I sighed happily and settled in for the short drive to the ranch, anticipating what the summer would bring.

Chapter 3

Innocence Lost

Gravel crunched under the tires as we turned into the dirt drive that led up to the ranch house. The old pickup coughed to a stop, and I leaped out the door, scrambling over Grandma's blue-checkered lap in my rush to get outside.

"Goodness, child! You'll be here all summer," she said. "If I didn't know better, I'd think you'd never been here before." Then to my grandfather, "It sure will be lively having a child around here, won't it, Al?"

"Sure will, Mavis," Grandpa agreed, his eyes crinkling at me from under the brim of his cowboy hat. "And after we get your things inside, I'll take you to the barn. Got a surprise waitin' for you."

"For me?" I said. Grandpa's surprises were always wonderful. "Come on, let's hurry!"

I grabbed the smallest of the suitcases from the back of the truck and dragged it to my new bedroom. My grandparents unloaded the bigger suitcase and my bag of stuffed animals; I couldn't possibly get through a summer without them.

The ranch house and immediate grounds were surrounded by three green hills. In front of the house stood the big brown barn where Grandpa kept his horse, Chiquita; two pet pigs, and a menacing Angus bull named George. Completing the farm were a black-and-white German shepherd named Pal and a golden collie named Lab. In addition to prunes, Grandpa raised cattle. His grazing land stretched out as far as the eye could see atop each of the three hills. Across the road was a second, larger barn, and covering the gentle slope directly behind the house was a thick eucalyptus grove where I loved to wander on lazy summer days. Apricot and apple trees dotted the ranch grounds, providing shade and quick snacks on the long afternoons.

After tossing my things in the closet, I pulled on my new cowboy boots and ran all the way to the barn where Grandpa was already waiting for me. I pushed the creaky barn door open and blinked as my eyes adjusted to the dark. The smell of fresh hay tickled my nose. Guided by the sight of Grandpa's hat, I tramped lightly to the last stall on the right.

He looked up with a silent smile as I approached the stall and then peered through the wooden slats.

"Oh, Grandpa! He's beautiful!" I breathed, fastening my eyes on the fuzzy, burnished hide of a calf.

"She, you mean," he winked at me. "And she's a Holstein-Friesian, a fine little calf. You can name her whatever you like."

Putting out a timid hand to stroke the soft fur, I dubbed her Clara on the spot. For the rest of the summer we were inseparable. I couldn't wake early enough each day to run down to the barn to see her. Here was something that was all mine. Something that loved me and depended on me for all its needs. After gulping down Grandma's hearty country breakfasts, I would spend as much time as possible with Clara, never returning to the snug little ranch house until the first stars peeked through the purple sky of dusk.

The long summer days passed quickly as I threw myself into ranch life—helping Grandpa with chores, picking apples for Grandma's pies, and talking to the animals, who seemed to understand me better than people did. Sometimes I took Clara to a huge alfalfa field near the ranch, where she would graze contentedly for hours while I strung wildflower necklaces for her. If I got sleepy, I'd head back to the barn, Clara trotting along behind me like one of the Pied Piper's children. The cool darkness was always refreshing after the hot afternoon sun. Burrowing down in the hay, my head on Clara's plump belly, I slept the blissful sleep of the innocent. But that innocence was not to last.

One morning at breakfast Grandpa announced he was going to start mending fences. It would be a lengthy, diffi-cult job, given the scope of his grazing land, and he needed to hire some help.

"But I can help you, Grandpa," I said eagerly. Grandpa chuckled.

"No, sweetheart, I'm afraid this is man's work, not work fit for a little girl." In the end he hired the son of a friend who lived in town, a short, stocky twenty-year-old named James who had greasy, black hair and an acne-scarred complexion. I had seen him once or twice before when I went into town with Grandpa to buy tools. Something about him gave me the willies. But he was always polite around my grandpa.

Toward the end of that first week of mending, Grandma told me to take some fresh-squeezed lemonade out to the men. It was late afternoon, and the temperature hovered in the nineties. I knew Grandpa and James were working in the south pasture, not too far from the house. I set off, holding the full tumblers carefully so as not to spill one drop.

I came to Grandpa first.

"Well, hello there," he said, taking off his hat and reaching for the ice-cold drink in my hand. "This sure does come in the nick of time. I'm parched."

After gulping down the lemonade, he handed me the empty tumbler and pointed to a few hundred yards away, where he said I would find James.

James was hammering and didn't hear me approach. But when he saw me, he grabbed the lemonade without a thank you and slurped it down loudly.

"There," he said, handing back the tumbler. "Looks like you don't have too much to keep you busy, little girl."

"My name's Robin," I said.

"Yeah, yeah, I know, Robin." He leaned back against the fence and eyed me closely.

"You know, you're kinda cute for a little snip of a girl. How old are you anyway?" I glanced up the hill to where Grandpa was working. A clump of trees blocked him from view. Deciding not to answer James, I turned to walk back toward the house. In a flash he pounced on me, wrestling me to the ground. His hands were all over me, tickling and touching me in places I knew he shouldn't be touching. "No. Stop it!" I said, struggling to fight him off. "Let me go!"

James finally let me up and leered at me as I snatched up

the tumblers and ran crying for home by way of another route.

Feeling scared and dirty, I stumbled into Clara's stall and clung to her soft, brown neck, sobbing. I hated James for what he had done to me, but the only one I could tell was my little calf.

The summer drew to a close in Napa Valley, and soon Grandma pulled out my suitcases for repacking. It was time to return home. After a tearful good-bye to Clara, I reluctantly got in the green pickup for the silent trip back to Vallejo.

Settling back in at home was difficult. Debbie was bossier than ever. The boys were wrapped up in their own worlds, with their own friends. My parents seemed too busy to notice me. Hadn't anyone missed me at all? I slouched in my bedroom all day, showing up only at mealtimes. School would start in two weeks. I hated even to think of it.

One night after dinner the doorbell rang. It was Grandma and Grandpa. In Grandpa's arms was a huge stuffed animal, a bright-green turtle. It was for me, he said. The four of us kids were thrilled with this unexpected visit. I soon learned it wasn't unexpected at all.

After romping around with Grandma and Grandpa, my brothers and sister were ushered out of the room. Only I was allowed to stay with the grown-ups. Something was up.

"Come over here and sit by me," Mom said, patting the seat cushion next to her. "I have something to ask you."

I glanced at the eyes of the three other adults in the room. Obviously they knew what Mom was about to say.

"First of all, Robin, I want you to know that your dad and I love you very much. We only want what's best for you.

We've given a lot of thought to what we're about to ask you." I waited for her to continue. "How would you like to live with Grandma and Grandpa?"

I stared at her, not really understanding what she meant.

"That way you could be with your calf Clara all the time," she said.

"You could join 4-H," Daddy interjected.

"And you could have your own room, and never have to worry about the neighborhood bullies again," Mom finished.

Then there was the matter of the Vallejo school system. The school officials had informed my parents I was so bright I should be skipped up to second grade. But the school system where my grandparents lived was more progressive, Mom explained. In Napa I could enter first grade and be with kids my own age, yet still be challenged enough not to get bored with school.

"So what do you think, Robin?" Dad said. "You don't have to go if you don't want to." All eyes turned on me, awaiting my reply. To my five-year-old mind it sounded too good to be true.

"I think I'd like to," I said matter-of-factly. And it was settled. Barely at home for a week and a half, I repacked my things—all my things this time—to return to the ranch with my grandparents.

On my last day at the house, when my grandparents and I were finally heading toward the door, Mom kissed me good-bye. Then she kneeled down, held me by the shoulders and looked at me tenderly. "Don't worry, sweetheart," she said. "You'll still see us all the time. We're just a few miles away."

Life at the ranch was good. I busied myself with school-work, ranch work, and participation in 4-H clubs. Because of my success in 4-H shows, I gradually gained confidence around my peers and became outgoing at school, though I still didn't have any real friends. Over the years I saw my family less and less. Weekends filled up for both my family and me, and the short distance between Napa and Vallejo suddenly stretched into lengthy miles. No problem. I would see the folks soon enough, I told myself.

But as time went by, I grew secretly angry and hurt that my parents never came for me. Why had they left me here so long? Sure, I was happy at the ranch, but if even once Mom had said, "Robin, come home; I love you and miss you," I would have rushed back to rejoin the family. As it was, I began to feel like a castoff.

My grandparents were good to me, but they never knew the inner turmoil I fought because I was "different." As far back as five years old I had been able to read people's minds. I would look at grown-ups and have a knowing. I saw things and felt things that no one else seemed to perceive. One day when I was about seven or eight I hiked out to the alfalfa field. Stretching out on the sweet-scented hillside, I suddenly burst into tears. No one knew me—the real me I had stuffed away in my heart. Maybe not even God, I thought to myself. I blinked up at the broad, blue sky and whispered, "When I grow up, I want to help people to feel." I didn't realize the weight of my words then, but God never forgot them.

During my first year at the ranch Grandma took a night job working at the switchboard of a mental hospital. Grandpa always went to the Taxpayers' Association on the third Friday night of every month, so on those evenings neither one could be at home with me. Grandpa decided that the best one to baby-sit me would be James, since he was often at the ranch to do odd jobs anyway. He and my grandmother had no way of knowing what James had done to me, and I was too ashamed to tell them.

"But, Grandpa, I don't like James," I pleaded when that first Friday night rolled around. "He always tries to tickle me. Can't you please take me with you?"

He was busy looking for his truck keys, so he didn't see the panic on my face.

"No, darling, I can't. Don't you worry, you'll be just fine. I'll be home by ten."

"Please, Grandpa, please" I said, tears filling my eyes. "Don't leave me."

This time my grandfather *did* look up at me but misread the fear in my eyes as distress over being left behind. For an answer, he gave me a big hug and assured me again he would be home by ten o'clock prompt.

I made a point of going to bed early that night. I couldn't bear the thought of sitting up watching TV with James.

My bedroom was dark, lighted only by feeble moonlight that filtered through the window. Grandma had given me my bath before leaving for work. Squeaky clean in my cotton jammies, I snuggled under the goose-down comforter, my mind skirting ever closer to dreamland.

Suddenly a noise at the door startled me awake. I blinked, my eyes struggling to make shapes out of the darkness. The door swung open, and a dark figure inched its way to the edge of my bed. Was it a burglar? Had the witch finally come to get me? Paralyzed with fear, I stared at the approaching horror. Just as the face leaned down close, the pale light from outside illuminated its features. I gasped, recognizing James.

"Just wanted to tuck you in," he snickered, sliding beneath the covers beside me. I tried to scramble off the bed, but he grabbed me in a headlock.

"And if you tell one living soul, I'll kill you," he hissed. In my childish naiveté, I believed him and kept the horror of his molesting to myself.

One time I did work up the nerve to tell Grandma I didn't want James to baby-sit me anymore, but I dared not tell her the reason why. Maybe she would understand.

"Oh, Robin, don't be silly," was all she said.

"But, Grandma, *I don't like James,*" I said fiercely, stamping my foot for emphasis.

Her head jerked up, a look of surprise on her face.

"Robin Harry, that's no way to talk about our good friend. Now I don't want to hear anything more about it."

And so James' crimes went undiscovered, and he crept into my bedroom once a month when he came to baby-sit me. His visits to my room were like clockwork, never failing. Feigning sleep was my only defense. Squeezing my eyes shut tight, I would imagine myself inside a little black box in my mind where he really couldn't touch me. Once inside this box, I started hearing voices.

"Come up here! Come up here with us!" the chorus of voices would say gleefully. "He can't get you here."

Eager to join these beckoning new friends, I would rise above my bed. I could see my physical self still in the bed, but my real self would rise up higher and higher until I was traveling around in space, surrounded by stars and darkness. One special place I went to was full of children—at least, I thought they were children. "You're special," they would tell me. "You're not like other people."

When it was over, and James had retreated to another part of the house, I would see myself coming back toward the earth. There was the ranch, with its brown barn and bushy treetops. There was the roof of the ranch house. Traveling through the roof, I could see myself lying in bed. And then I was back in bed, inside my body again. A gold, shimmery thread connected me to my body, and the "children" told me never to let go of it. It was my connection. I somehow knew that if I lost that, I would lose myself.

As these out-of-body experiences continued, my mind became more open to hear things and know other people's thoughts. I was hearing voices nearly all the time at this point, but I thought it was my own mind speaking to me. At age seven, while I was attending 4-H camp, I met one of my brother Bobby's friends. John was very cute. He was also twelve years old. I watched as he and his girlfriend sauntered around the campgrounds arm in arm, flaunting their romance. I sized the girl up. She wasn't so gorgeous, I sniffed. Everyone said I was turning into a beauty.

"You could have him," a voice said, "He could be y*our* boyfriend."

"You're right," I said, answering the voice out loud. I decided that someday I would be the one on John's arm. Over the next few years I saw John from time to time because of his friendship with Bobby. "When you grow up, we'll date," he would say, winking at me confidentially. Sure enough, when I was fourteen—and he nineteen—we did date. He was my steady boyfriend for four years.

By the time I was twelve I had figured out that James wasn't really going to kill me if I talked, but now shame kept me silent. Soon I would no longer need a baby sitter, but James would still come to the ranch to work. I decided I was old enough to make sure he never had a chance to bother me again. One day I found the courage to call Mom and tell her I wanted to come home. She wondered at the urgency in my voice, and why the sudden decision, but she and Dad came to pick me up the very next day, no questions asked.

I was glad to be part of the family once more, but at the same time, my mother and I had frequent confrontations. At the ranch I had been allowed to speak my mind and express my feelings. But at home that free expression just sounded like back talk to my mother.

I finished out my school years in Vallejo. The confidence I had gained from 4-H served me well, and I continued to blossom socially. At age fifteen I was an honor student, homecoming queen, head cheerleader, head majorette, Miss Solano County, and voted by my classmates as most likely to succeed. I had plenty of attention from boys and was well received by the girls at school, but I still had no close friends.

During the summer of 1972, two months before my junior year, I was selected to travel to England with a group of students. It was there, in England, that I had my first taste of how frighteningly real the psychic realm can be.

Chapter 4

Midnight Visitation

J brushed back a lock of hair and peered out the misty window. A light drizzle dappled the ancient cobblestone pathways of King's College, and the iron-gray sky lent a bleak cast to the world. Only yesterday our group of students and counselors had landed at Heathrow airport and made the trip out to the college, where we would be staying. Even as the bus sloshed through the streets of London, I had felt something strange come over me. Probably just jet lag, I told myself. But this morning I still couldn't shake off the feeling. An indefinable weakness permeated my body. I glanced around the anti-quated dorm room and wondered how many lives had passed through its walls before me.

Firm rapping at the door brought me out of my reverie. "Coming!" I shouted as I picked up my purse.

It was Katrina, a girl I had met on the flight over from California. Although only sixteen, one year older than I was, she seemed to possess an adult-like authority that was unnerving—intriguing. Her father was one of the parent counselors on the trip. Seeing the chemistry between the two of us, he had arranged to have our rooms next to each other.

"We've gotta hurry. The bus is leaving in five minutes," Katrina said, slipping something into her jacket pocket.

"What's that?" I asked.

"Just my tarot cards," she said, "Come on, I'll show them to you later."

The ride out to Stratford-on-Avon was filled with pleasant chit-chat and the rich scenery of the English countryside. As we talked, I felt a growing kinship with Katrina. And when the conversation turned to the paranormal, I knew I had at last found someone like me.

"Katrina, have you ever, you know, heard voices or anything?" I stammered, thinking how absurd my question must have sounded.

Her expression was almost indifferent as she looked me in the eye and said, "Of course. All the time."

During the bus ride we had left dreary weather behind, and now, as we pulled into Shakespeare's famous birthplace, a sunny sky spread a golden hue on everything. The group filed out of the bus and split off into little tour groups of three and four. We had two hours to sightsee before the trip back to the college.

"Hey, why don't we start with Anne Hathaway's cottage," I suggested to my newfound friend and her father.

"Sounds good to me," Mr. Holmes said, turning to lead us in the direction of the cottage. We strolled through the manicured garden that led to the entrance of the cottage, then stepped inside. Cool, dank air and the stillness of centuries enclosed us as we wandered through the rooms.

Fascinated with history, I soon found myself separated

from Katrina and her father. Back in the front hall I started up the staircase to the second floor. No other tourists were there. My attention was drawn to a large, desktop bookcase with glass-paned, hinged doors. I stepped up close to read the book titles, my breath leaving fog on the panes. Two gilded books with green leather bindings lay open on the desk. LOOK BUT DO NOT TOUCH, PLEASE, a small placard read.

As I leaned down to read the ancient print, suddenly my ears closed up, shutting out all sound of the natural world around me. In the manner of a camera zooming in on something, my eyes riveted on a single word written on the page. It was my name. No, this can't be. I thought, my chest tightening. But somehow the other words on the yellowed pages had blurred from sight. ROBIN. ROBIN. ROBIN. The sound of my name echoed in my head. Terrified, I backed away from the bookcase and bumped into the wall next to the staircase.

I winced at the jarring bump, then looked down the staircase. What my eyes saw there didn't make sense. A little girl in a long, white nightgown was falling backward down the steep incline.

"Help me! Help me!" she screamed, her arms outstretched, her eyes pleading. I watched in horror as she landed with a thump at the bottom, apparently lifeless.

"No," I shook my head, covering my face with my hands. "This can't be real." But it had seemed all too real, as if I had just witnessed the death of a child. I started sobbing.

Someone grabbed me around the waist. I gasped, looking up. It was only Katrina. Limp as a rag doll, I let her lead me downstairs. Although my mind was reeling, I remembered to glance down at the foot of the stairs. "Where is she?" I mumbled. The little girl was gone.

I blinked at the brightness as we emerged from the cottage. Katrina led me to a bench in the garden, and I slumped down, trying to get a grip on myself. It was no use. I couldn't stop shaking. Katrina put her arm around me comfortingly.

"I see what you see," she whispered.

I looked up at her face, puzzled. "You what?"

"I see what you see," she repeated. "I see the little girl. I see the long, white nightgown. I see her falling down the stairs."

"But what *was* it?" I said. "Things like that aren't supposed to happen."

"But they do," a man's voice said. I looked up and saw Mr. Holmes standing there, his face wearing a mingled look of concern and fascination.

Taking the seat beside me, he adopted a fatherly tone and patted my shoulder. "It's all right, Robin. This area is full of spiritual presences. Now tell me what you saw."

I did. When I had finished, he said, "You probably lived here in another life. Perhaps that little girl was you."

This was all too strange, yet, with no invitation from me, the supernatural had been intruding on my life since I was five years old.

On the ride back to Kings College, Mr. Holmes talked candidly, excitedly, of the psychic realm and what it meant for those chosen to be a part of it. It was from him that I first learned the term *New Age*.

"Sometimes I just wish it would all go away," I sighed, having had enough of the topic. Mr. Holmes just smiled and said nothing, his eyes glittering. *All in good time*, his eyes seemed to say. *All in good time.*

That night, after a late dinner, I settled into my dorm room, not feeling up to the little social hour most of the other students were attending. I read for a while, then turned out the light. I needed a good night's sleep. Perhaps by tomorrow I would feel better.

The night wore on, and I slept fitfully, troubled by disturbing dreams. Suddenly a loud THWACK! jolted me awake. The double, hinged window across the room had opened, banging against the wall. Pale light from the moon illuminated the dingy curtains, giving them a surreal whiteness. My breath came in short, rapid gasps. Goosebumps crept over the length of my body, and I shivered. It was then I realized the temperature in the room had dropped to an icy chill too cold for a summer night, even in England.

I stared at the window. I knew something was in my room.

Somehow I got up and knocked on Katrina's door. I told her what had happened, stark fear distorting my features. She listened silently until I had finished the horrible account.

"You can't let these spirits control you," she said matter-of-factly. Katrina brushed past me and walked into my room. She shut the window with authority.

"You've got to take authority over these spirits or they'll torment you, Robin," she said. "Now, why don't you come back to my room and sleep in there. I'll protect you."

I was only too eager to comply. Grabbing my pillow and a quilt, I hurried out of the frigid room and made a pallet on the floor beside Katrina's bed. Oddly enough, I finished the night in a deep, sound sleep.

Morning came, and with it an introduction to Katrina's tarot cards.

"Come over here," she said, patting the bed beside her. "It's time I taught you how to do this."

After that disturbing day and night, all went normal on the trip. Three weeks later we flew back to California and parted company, each student to his own town. I never saw Katrina again.

Chapter 5

Stalked

San Luis Obispo is a sleepy little town surrounded by golden brown, rolling hills. Each fall thousands of college students invade the quiet town, filling it with laughter, football games, campus parties, and dreams.

I had my own share of dreams as I roared out of the driveway in my red '66 Mustang and waved good-bye to Mom and Dad and the little peach house in Vallejo. As I turned the corner at the bottom of the street, adrenaline surged through my veins, and I let out a loud party whoop.

"Free at last, Mickey!" I said, glancing back at the giant, plush Mickey Mouse on the back seat. Sitting next to him was a fluffy rabbit as tall as I was and the huge green turtle Grandpa and Grandma had given me all those years ago. Even these silent friends seemed to be smiling as we rode off together toward our new adventure. College! It was September 1975.

I had decided on California Polytechnic State University for a simple reason: it was where John, my longtime boyfriend, had enrolled. I didn't know it then, but our four-year courtship would fizzle out within three months of college life. The availability of so many different girls was too much a temptation for him.

Six hours, and a hamburger and chocolate malt later, I drove through the gates of "CM Poly," as it was nicknamed, gawking at the Ivy League brick buildings that dotted the shady campus. Everywhere I looked students were unloading cars, playing Frisbee, and toting their possessions up the stately staircases that led to their dormitories. I pulled up in front of McClaren Hall and parked.

After dragging my things inside, I found room number 228 and pushed it open with my hip. Sitting in the dorm was a somewhat overweight girl about my age. Her dark hair and olive complexion hinted at Mediterranean ancestry. As I struggled inside, she looked up from the magazine on her lap.

"Hi. I'm Jill," she said. "Looks like we'll be roomies."

I returned her warm smile. "I'm Robin. Nice to meet you." Something told me we would get along just fine.

Life at school jumped off to a good start. Since I had always loved to write poetry, I decided to major in journalism. During that first week Jill and I rushed for the same sorority and were accepted.

One day toward the end of the first semester, I was walking down the street on my way to class when I heard a loud whistle behind me. I turned around, but no one was there. *That's strange*, I thought. *I know I heard it.* Something about the whistle sent prickly sensations up the back of my neck.

The very next day, as I walked to class, I heard the same whistle. Again, no one was there. This strange phenomenon occurred for several days in a row. I began to expect the eerie whistle whenever I walked alone. Along with the whistle came the unsettling feeling that someone was following me. I found myself glancing over my shoulder all the time.

It was early December, and the crisp California air woke me to a beautiful, sunny day. I dressed for my first class, then grabbed my books.

"Hi, Janey!" I called out to a sorority sister as I skipped, lighthearted, down the large front steps of McClaren Hall. In just two more weeks I would have completed my first semester at college.

Since I was running late, I decided to take a shortcut down a shady side street. Sunlight peeping through the canopy of trees overhead made lacy patterns on the asphalt. My mind was completely at ease, running over thoughts of the upcoming holidays. Then it happened.

That horrible whistle.

This time the whistle seemed insistent. My heart pounded, and a sense of dread seized me. Somehow I knew that when I turned around this time, someone—or something—would be there.

Turning slowly, my eyes locked onto a robe-clad figure standing a few yards away from me. I looked around and realized that no one else could see him. I stared at the strange apparition.

"I must be having a psychic vision or something," I muttered out loud. The figure remained silent and staring, his cold blue eyes peering out from a face that looked alien. He was around eight feet tall and wore a long, white robe that hung to his feet. His white, shoulder-length hair was brushed back from his forehead, revealing strange features set in tightly stretched skin.

I stood frozen in place, still not convinced that what I saw was real.

"I'm here to help you," he said in a monotone voice. "I've been watching you since you were a small child."

Suddenly my feet felt free to move, and I took off running, repeating the prayer that had sustained me through my young life.

"Our Father, which art in heaven, hollowed be Thy name. Thy kingdom come, Thy will be done...." I kept praying as I ran.

That night, as I tried to sleep, I sensed someone in my room. When I opened my eyes, the robe-clad figure was hovering in midair over the foot of my bed. I tried to scream out, but a muffled groan was all that escaped my throat. I glanced at Jill's bed; she was sound asleep. I was in this alone.

I shook myself hard, trying to make it go away.

"You're not dreaming," the figure said, reading my mind. "I've come to help you." His steel-blue eyes bored into me. When had I seen those eyes before?

"I am a celestial spirit assigned to you," he continued. "I have come to aid you in your destiny and teach you about the coming New Age." He paused. I lay stock-still, listening.

"I am part of a group of twelve beings who live in a higher spiritual plane. We are more advanced than earth people, and we have been cultivating and releasing information into the earth for thousands of years. The counsel of twelve is responsible for releasing this higher knowledge and always chooses individuals who have certain abilities to be releasers of this information. We've been watching you. We have taken notice of your special gifts. Now it is time for me to teach you." The spirit paused again, waiting for me to absorb his words.

"Remember when you were a child and you used to leave your body? I was there. I was in that special place. I've known you all your life, and now it is time for us to merge energies." I thought back to those terror-filled nights of my childhood when James molested me and I flew above my bed, through the ceiling and up to a special playground in the sky. It was like being in Never-Never Land with Peter Pan and the "lost children." I vaguely remembered having conversations with one "child" in particular who seemed to be especially interested in me.

As quickly as he had come, he disappeared again, leaving me staring into the blank space where he had been.

"Dear God," I whispered, clutching the sheets up to my chin. "This can't be happening to me."

Since that frightening vision at Anne Hathaway's cottage three years earlier, I had made a conscious decision to block out the psychic realm. Or at least the dark side of it. Without any Christian foundation to build on, I mistakenly lumped all supernatural phenomena under the vague term "God." But there were positive and negative forces to the supernatural universe, I reasoned. Surely God was the positive energy. The other stuff...well, I didn't really know what to do with it. Because I had been successful at shutting it out for three years, this encounter with the hideous spirit threw me for a loop.

Dawn has a way of lessening the terrors of the night. The next morning I found myself driven by curiosity to find out more about what was happening to me. I went to the university library and looked up books on psychic encounters. For hours on end I would sit cross-legged on the floor of the narrow book aisles, a pile of dusty books around me. I worked my way through each one of them, gobbling up the new information. Once, as I sat reading, my head bowed in deep concentration over a book, I glanced up and saw the spirit standing at the far end of the aisle between the cluttered bookshelves. We stared at each other a moment, then he was gone.

Through my research I learned, to my relief, that many people had the same experiences I had. These celestial spirits were called spirit guides, and they were supposed to elevate a person into greater realms of spirituality. The people who have these encounters are normally very sensitive. Some of the more sensitive ones are called mediums. I began to believe that possibly I was a medium. Armed with this new knowledge, I was not as frightened of the spirit anymore, though he still appeared only randomly.

Other psychic things began to happen. Just as when I was a child, I could look into someone's eyes and hear their thoughts. Sometimes I would walk into a room and see a vision of something that took place there years before. And not all the things that I experienced were pleasant.

During the few months at school I had befriended a guy named Jack who played for the college volleyball team. One day he called me and asked me to come over for dinner.

"You gotta check out this place," he said, referring to the new house he had rented off-campus. "You'll love it."

"Sounds great," I said. "I'll be there in twenty minutes."

I hopped in my Mustang and drove through the tree-lined streets that led to Jack's house. A tingling sensation spread over my body, and my stomach felt unsettled. The nearer I got to my destination, the more nauseated I became. As I pulled up in front of the ivy-covered wooden house, anxiety clawed at my insides. Small beads of perspiration formed on my forehead. When Jack opened the door, my eyes riveted on something behind him. It was the body of a woman, crumpled on the floor in a patch of blood stained carpet. My knees gave out, and I started to faint.

"Robin, are you ok?" Jack's voice asked, seeming to come from far away. He tried to help me inside the house.

"No!" I screamed, fearing the violent energies I was sensing. "Who is that woman?" Then my entire body collapsed. Jack caught me in time, sat me down on the front steps and peered inquiringly into my eyes.

"Robin, what are you talking about?" he said, his face drawn with concern.

"I saw a woman lying on the floor, dead." I could tell by the look on his face that he was not seeing what I was seeing.

"There is no woman there, Robin, calm down," he said, but his voice sounded uneasy.

I was shaken and sticky with sweat. On top of that, I was concerned that at any moment I would vomit.

We sat for a moment in silence.

"I think I might know what you saw," Jack said quietly.

I looked up at him eagerly, hoping he might be able to explain.

"When I came here to rent the house, there was a reddish stain on the carpet. I asked the owner what it was, and she told me they would be putting in new carpet before I moved in. She never told me what it was. The day after I moved in a neighbor dropped by to see me."

"Well, go on," I said. "Don't leave me hanging."

"He told me about the horrible murder that had taken place in this house. A woman had been killed with a double-barreled shotgun right in my living room."

I took a deep breath and tried to gain my composure.

"But how did you see? I mean, how did you know—"

I cut him off in mid-sentence and gave him some hurried explanation.

"Look, I've gotta go. I'm sorry, Jack." I walked on shaky legs back to my car and roared away. When I looked in my rearview mirror, Jack was still sitting there on the steps, staring after me with a troubled expression.

I drove back to my dorm feeling weak and emotionally upset. Once inside my dorm room, I lay down on the bed and closed my eyes, hoping to make the bad feeling go away.

"It's part of the territory."

I sat up. The spirit was in my room, standing by the window. "What?" I said angrily.

"It comes with the gift. Not everything is going to be sweet, pretty, and tingly," he said with a grimace. His face looked imposingly evil.

"Get out of here!" I shouted. "Leave me alone!" Within a split second he disappeared. But I knew he would be back, sooner or later.

Chapter 6

Searching for Answers

*S*ighing loudly, I slapped the textbook on my lap
closed. "What's the matter?" Jill asked, glancing up
from her desk.

"Oh, nothing. I just can't seem to concentrate, that's all,"
I said lightly, avoiding her eyes. The truth was, my mind felt
too open. I could hear the spirit more than my own
thoughts, even though I tried to shut him out. Every time
he appeared he looked more evil than the time before, and
he had become increasingly abrupt and short-tempered
with me. Several months had passed since my first
encounter with the spirit, and I had been unsuccessful at
mastering control of his presence. I struggled to get my own
thoughts back, but they were always overpowered. My
schoolwork had suffered. Soon I feared I would be forced to
drop out of college altogether.

"Is it because of him?" Jill ventured.

My head snapped up. "Who?"

"You know who, Robin. That spirit you've been telling
me about. Is it because of him?"

"All right, all right," I said curtly. "So it is the spirit. But what do you think *I* can do about it? It isn't as if I asked for all this garbage." Jill played with her pencil before answering.

"Maybe it is your fault."

"Oh, come on, Jill. How can you say that?"

"Robin, I only know what I see. You've been getting, well, *weird* lately. You never come to any sorority functions anymore, and everyone's worried about you. All you do is go to class, hole up in the library and sleep. And that's another thing. At night, sometimes I hear you go out in the hall and talk to that thing. I don't know, Robin, it's just creepy. Why don't you lay off the psychic stuff for a while, huh?"

My eyes bored into hers, searching for any underlying motive in what she said. Satisfied of her sincerity, I shrugged and said, "Maybe I'll talk to a professional about it. A psychologist or something. Don't worry about me, Jill," I added, forcing a smile. "I'll be fine."

But I wasn't. I only grew worse. My appetite dropped off to nothing, and I wasn't getting any sleep at night. My physical health was undermined by persistent headaches, nausea, dizziness, and severe panic attacks. As that first school year drew to a close, I knew I had to do something.

The address scrawled across the scrap of paper in my hand matched the numbers on the log frame bungalow. Yes, this was the place. My search for help had taken me to the office of Dr. Pinder, a psychology professor. Several faculty offices were clustered in these rustic bungalows under the trees. I had always seen the cute little buildings and wondered what they were. Now I was stepping through the door of one, hoping to find help inside.

After a brief wait in the makeshift lobby, a tall, thin man

with salt-and-pepper hair, wire-rimmed glasses and a trim beard opened the door to the inner office.

"Miss Harry?" he inquired.

I jumped up. "Yes, that's me."

"Come right in, please," he said, gesturing politely with his hand.

I settled into an easy chair and looked around the cramped office. Piles of books were everywhere. He opened the blinds to brighten the room, then took his seat behind the desk, leaning forward on propped-up elbows. On the phone I had told him about my psychic encounters, and now he stared at me like a rat ready to pounce on a piece of ripe cheddar cheese. I squirmed uncomfortably. "Well, let's get started, shall we? I want you to look at these pieces of paper and tell me what you see."

Spread before me were several sheets of paper with ink blots on them. I studied them for a minute.

"Well, I see a butterfly in this one. This one over here looks like a dog, and this one looks like two people kissing."

He nodded. "Uh-hmmm, go on, go on." After several hours of this type of testing, he looked up at me and said, "There's nothing wrong with you, child. In fact, there is everything right with you."

I was stunned and not a little irritated at this point. I glared at him, waiting for some possible explanation of what he meant.

"You're psychic," he said triumphantly.

"Bingo," came my sarcastic retort.

"The undiscovered frontier," Dr. Pinder went on, ignoring my rudeness. "You've been enlightened. Your mind has been expanded to higher realms of consciousness."

"Doctor," I said, running out of patience, "What I want to know is, how do I get unexpanded?"

"No, child, this is a gift. You need to learn to control it. Once you master it, it will be a great asset to you. I'm going to set up an appointment for you to see Dr. Lands. He's a friend of mine, and he's had quite a bit of experience in this area."

Several days later I found myself in another bungalow sitting across the desk from Dr. Lands, a psychology professor who dabbled in parapsychology. The walls of his office were papered with certificates and degrees, and stacks of books covered most of the available desk and floor space.

Dr. Lands resembled a scarecrow with his lanky limbs poking out from too-short sleeves and pant legs. Stringy black hair dripped off his forehead like licorice, and his eyes squinted at me from behind Coke-bottle lenses.

"So you're Robin," he said eagerly, as if that in itself was something special. "Do you know what being psychic sensitive means?"

"Well, I've read Edgar Cayce's books, but I don't know a whole lot about it," I said.

Dr. Lands also put me through a series of tests.

He held up flashcards that had numbers and shapes on one side—the side facing him—and blank white on the other side. My task was to "read" the cards as best I could.

"Can you tell me what this is?" he said, holding up the first card. I closed my eyes and instantly received the image in my mind.

"It's a triangle," I said.

"And this," he said, flipping to the next card.

"The number four."

I got all of the flashcards right. Next Dr. Lands told me that if I could "see" the colors of the shapes, it would mean I was really advanced. Again, I succeeded.

Obviously pleased, he grilled me on everything from my background to the guiding spirit, as he called it. He wanted to know all about it. What did it look like? When had I first known the spirit was trying to contact me? Had I had any contact with departed relatives?

As I talked on, I felt the spirit enter the room behind me. By now I could converse with it in my mind, though I had begun to be fearful of it. I looked over my shoulder at the imposing figure in white.

"What's he doing? Is he here? Is he saying anything?" Dr. Lands asked excitedly.

"You can't shut me out, Robin," the spirit said. "You and I are meant to be one. You belong to me. The universe can be touched by you."

"He's telling me that I can't shut him out," I relayed to the foolish-looking professor, who was practically drooling in his excitement. "He also says the universe can be touched by me."

"Ask him what he means by the universe being touched."

The spirit didn't wait for me to ask. "Tell the doctor that a quantum leap in the consciousness of man is coming to the whole earth, and that you have been chosen to assist us in our mission to bring the whole earth into one mind, one religion—the New Age."

"You tell him yourself," I spat at the spirit, who had moved to face me. "Choose someone else. I don't care about energy-level alterations or leaps or jumps. I just want out."

I hurled a look of disgust at Dr. Lands and hurried from

the room.

The days dragged on torturously. Nights were even worse. Was there no escape from this menacing spirit, whose eyes bored into my very soul? I had tried doctors. I had tried willpower. What else was left? One evening, as I lay listlessly in bed, I remembered meeting the campus pastor during an interview for the college newspaper. Perhaps he could help me.

The next morning I called for an appointment. He could fit me in that day, he said. Somehow I made it through my classes, having this hope to hold onto. At 2 p.m. I entered the front door of the campus ministries office, which had been converted from a private home. The living room area served as a large meeting hall with stackable chairs lined up in rows. Against the far right wall sat an upright piano, its ivory keys yellowed with age. A sign directed me down the hall to the minister's office, where a smiling, grandmotherly secretary sat at a desk.

"Just go on in, dear. He'll be here in a minute," she said, motioning me to the pastor's office. I took a seat in a burgundy leather chair and glanced around the walls, which were covered in dark wood paneling. Behind the minister's desk hung an ornate, gilt-framed portrait of Jesus. I stared at the face with its soft, searching eyes. The sight of those gentle eyes made me burst into tears.

"Hello, are you Robin?" said a voice behind me. Quickly wiping my eyes, I turned to see Pastor Graves entering the room. "I'm terribly sorry I'm late. Now, what can I do for you?"

He was as kind as I had remembered. Knowing this might be my last chance at help, I poured out the events of the past several months, barely stopping to breathe. As my bizarre tale unfolded, the pastor shifted nervously in his high-backed leather chair. He glanced here and there around the room, seldom looking me in the eye.

He cleared his throat, "Tell me again what Dr. Lands said." He knew of Dr. Lands and his research into paranormal activity.

"He said I'm a psychic and that this is a gift I have to learn to control. But, Pastor, I don't want to control it. I want to get rid of it. Can you help me?"

By now the pastor was downright fidgety. When he did look at me, I thought I saw fear in his eyes. Years later I realized he must have sensed the presence of evil around me and felt helpless to deal with it.

"Pastor," I went on, "I think this psychic stuff runs in my family. I have always had this recurring dream about—"

"I'm sorry," he said, standing to his feet. "I think we'll have to continue this another time."

Chapter 7

A Spirit Named Marilyn

As I hiked up the mountain behind my dorm, I knew something had to happen soon or I would lose my mind. It was late spring, and nature was in full bloom, but the beauty of the outer world made a mockery of the turmoil within my mind. I thought of people locked up in insane asylums who constantly talk to the empty air as if carrying on a conversation with someone that nobody else can see. I didn't want to be like that. I shuddered as I approached the mountaintop clearing, the students called "the slab."

The slab was a large piece of concrete out in the middle of the forest surrounded by tall evergreens. Perhaps it was the abandoned foundation for a hillside home that never took shape, but the slab now made a perfect place for meditation, which I took very seriously now and practiced twice a day. It was my only escape from the confusion my life had become. I sat down in my usual meditative position and let the sunlight bathe my tanned shoulders with golden warmth. Everything felt so peaceful. Only the sounds of nature reached my ears: birds chirping, a breeze whispering through the lofty evergreen boughs, the soft rustling of some woodland animal in the thicket nearby.

I emptied my mind and opened myself up to become one with the trees, the sky, the sun, the universe. I felt light and free, my senses heightened and receiving. As I sat there, lost in the tranquility, I heard a voice that I knew was not human. But it did not belong to my robe-clad tormenter either.

"I will help you. Come with me. Come up with me higher." The voice sounded soft, feminine.

"Who are you?" I asked.

"I am Marilyn. I have come to save you from the evil that has tried to destroy you." Attracted by the comforting voice, I allowed myself to go deeper into this new state of consciousness.

"The evil came to hurt you," it said. "He is from the dark side. Stay with me, and he will not harm you."

Suddenly a brilliant white light hovered over me like a spotlight. *This must be Marilyn*, I thought.

"God is us. We are God. There are good energies, and there are evil energies. What you open yourself up to is what you become."

My mind seemed to be speaking on its own, whispering secret truths that could liberate me from evil. Could this be the refuge I had so long been seeking? Had I at last found one who would comfort me, not torment me? I sighed and lay back on the warm concrete. Yes. This was right. This was good. I was free, and he—that awful spirit—was gone. In his place was a spirit that called itself Marilyn.

After about twenty more minutes in communion with

Marilyn, I hurried back down the mountain to the dorm. I couldn't wait to tell Jill the good news.

The school year finished on a high note. My life was transformed, and everyone seemed to notice it. I was calm and at peace with myself and the world around me. As Marilyn and I became better acquainted, she guided me through hours of deep meditation, always leading me to "higher" realms of spirituality. Within a few months I was able to see an image of Marilyn in my mind whenever I meditated. At other times she made her presence known only through her voice. I grew to trust the gentle, lilting voice that seemed infinitely wiser than me.

One day I passed the gym on my way to the journalism building and saw a dance class in progress. Something about the movement of the dancers made me stop and gaze through the large front window. The petite instructor looked like a real-life version of Betty Boop. Her enthusiasm was contagious.

"You want to be a dancer, don't you?" said the voice inside my head, reading my thoughts. "You can," the voice continued. "You *can* be a dancer." The scene mesmerized me—the mirrors, the beat of the music, the rows of sweaty dancers in leotards and leg-warmers.

The dance instructor looked up from her warmup routine, and our eyes connected. She walked right up to me and said the words I had just heard in my head.

"You want to be a dancer, don't you?" she asked.

Hearing these words out loud ignited something deep in my heart, and tears filled my eyes. It was all the answer she needed.

"I can make you a professional dancer in four years if you

are willing to give me twenty hours a week. Think about it."
And she walked back to rejoin her class.

The very next day I was on the front row of that class,
sweating along with everyone else. I had found my niche.

Dancing became a passion with me, and I threw myself
into it head first. Somehow I fit in two hours of dance class
at college every day. Plus, after I got off work from the ice
cream parlor where I waitressed, I headed straight for the
instructor's of-campus dance studio and trained from five
o'clock until 10:30 p.m. The hard work paid off. Gradually I
watched my curvy figure transform into the angular body
of a professional dancer.

At the end of the first quarter of dance, each student had
to choreograph a complete dance routine for the final exam.
I worked extra hard on my routine and even costumed it to
give it professional polish. When my turn came to perform,
the other students cleared the floor. I could see Jackie, the
instructor, watching from the back of the room, her eyes
intent on me. The music came up, and my body flowed
into rhythm as if I and the music were one. I danced and
whirled and strutted, bringing every note of the music to
life through the movements of my body. When I finished
the routine, the other dancers broke into spontaneous
cheers.

I glanced at Jackie. Her face was beaming.

Sweating from the exertion, I made my way past the
other dancers to the water fountain in the hallway.

Someone tapped me on the shoulder. It was Jackie.
Before I could ask how she liked my routine, she handed me
a folded slip of paper and stepped back into the classroom. I
nervously unfolded the little note, which contained my

grade and only three words:

A+++

Let's have lunch!

It was three days before Jackie could arrange to meet me. I arrived at the little campus snack bar twenty minutes early and selected a table outside on the shady veranda. At 12:30 I spotted her coming up the sidewalk through a crowd of students. I hailed her, and she waved back, quickly joining me at the table for two.

"Hello there," I said. "I took the liberty of ordering you a Coke. Hope you don't mind."

"Oh, that's great," Jackie said in her typical breathless manner. "For a while I thought I'd never be able to get away, but here I am."

After a few minutes of chit-chat over sizzling cheeseburgers and fries, the conversation turned serious. Jackie pushed her plate to the side and leaned forward, arms crossed on the table.

"Robin, tell me, what are your aspirations?" she said. "I've never seen a dance student progress so rapidly before."

"Well, as you know, I've been majoring in journalism, but that day you told me I could be a dancer, something happened in my heart." I looked down and played with my napkin, blinking hard. "When you said that, I almost wanted to cry."

Jackie's eyes sparkled. "You have a gift. You should use it." After a pause she went on, "Look, I've got a dance company that performs at a disco. I'm looking for another dancer. Interested?"

"Are you serious?" I said, only half believing what I had heard. "Nobody gets to dance professionally after just three or four months of training."

"You're not just anybody," Jackie smiled. "I know a good dancer when I see one. What do you say?"

I almost laughed out loud with joy. "I'll take it!"

Half an hour later, as I walked back to my dorm, Marilyn spoke to me. "See? I told you you could do it."

I smiled, hugged my purse to my chest and flew up the stairs of McClaren Hall, taking them two at a time.

Chapter 8

Ticket to Hollywood

Thick fog obscured the highway as I drove westward toward Hollywood in the pale light of dawn that spring morning of 1979. I could hardly believe I was on my way there after training so hard for so long. Leaning my head against the headrest, I reflected back over the past four years. With Marilyn constantly driving me, I had developed into an excellent dancer—top quality television material. I had also studied voice and acting, and the experience in Jackie's dance company had molded me into a precision performer. Now I was on my way to my first professional dance audition to see how I could compete with the best in the business.

In one month I would graduate from college with a degree in journalism, but I had decided to put that on the shelf for a career in show business, in which Marilyn had promised would make me a star....

My stomach jittery, I gripped the steering wheel until my knuckles turned white. *Stay calm*, I told myself, breathing deeply. *Don't get tense, or you'll never be able to dance today.*

As I rounded a curve, I heard Marilyn speaking in my mind. "Today you will get this job, and it will be your ticket to Los Angeles. Many other things are about to line up. Just go with the flow, and do as I tell you. All things are being made ready in the spirit."

"Yes, Marilyn," I said. The sound of her voice boosted my confidence. She had never failed me yet.

Five hours later I pulled up in front of the Debbie Reynolds Studio in North Hollywood. Cars were crammed into every conceivable parking space around the large warehouse facility. Leotard-clad dancers filed into the studio carrying oversized dance bags stuffed with dancewear, jazz shoes, tap shoes, ballet shoes, leg warmers and other dance paraphernalia. Some of the girls whispered with friends as they approached the double doors. Others walked alone in silence. Still sitting in the car, I glanced around at my fellow dancers and smiled to myself. I had inside information.

The audition room was immense. I was surprised to see how many girls there were, probably 500–600. Someone motioned to me to grab a number and get in line.

The music started, and everyone watched as two dancers, the choreographer's assistants, performed the routine. The choreographer entered through a door at the far end of the cavernous room, cigarette in one hand and clipboard in the other. He acknowledged this and that dancer. The rest of us looked on with envy recognizing that these were the pros.

I checked my appearance in the mirror, then lifted my chin a little higher. What did I have to worry about? Didn't I already know what the outcome would be? Still, a twinge of doubt flickered in my mind.

The assistants called out number after number, group

after group. Each group had to learn the routine and then dance it for the choreographer. After they had finished, he lined them up and walked in front of them like a Marine sergeant, scrutinizing them from head to toe.

Each girl held her breath as the choreographer either gave a curt nod "yes" or shook his head "no."

The group with my number was called, and I stepped forward confidently. I had already learned the routine just by watching from the sidelines. When the music came up, I flowed through every motion effortlessly.

I felt the choreographer's eyes on me as I danced, one step, another step, a turn, a kick—all with a brilliant smile, of course.

When the music stopped, he lined us up and walked directly over to me.

"Have I seen you before?" he asked.

"No, I've never worked with you," I said, coyly implying I had worked for many others, just never him.

I could sense Marilyn's presence.

After a moment of thought, he nodded his head "yes," and my heart somersaulted inside my chest. I had made it!

The choreographer finished his grueling six hour audition and lined up the eight dancers he had chosen. He thanked all the others for coming and asked them to leave. He had made his decision. Hundreds of crestfallen girls picked up their dance bags and walked out the door.

I stood next to one of those dancers the choreographer had acknowledged on the way in.

"Hi, I'm Robin," I whispered. She glanced knowingly at me and smiled. "This is your first job, huh?"

I nodded and smiled back.

The choreographer began to lay out the details of the job. Each of us would sign a one-year contract to dance on all the country and western television specials for the producer of "Solid Gold."

Having landed the job, all that remained for me to do was to go back to San Luis Obispo, collect my degree, load up my car and head to Hollywood—for good this time.

I had already started packing in my head. "Thank you, Marilyn," I whispered.

Within a few weeks I moved to Hollywood and rented an apartment located right underneath the famous Hollywood sign on the hill. My first night in the apartment I sat on the balcony, a cool drink in my hand, and gazed up at the huge block letters that seemed painted in stardust across the black sky. What would Grandpa think of his little Robin now? I had come so far in such a short time. And it was only the beginning. Tomorrow was my first rehearsal for the new "Country Top Twenty" job. Closing my eyes, I listened to the rhythmic sound of palm fronds rustling in the warm Pacific breeze.

That night Marilyn appeared to me in a dream. Up until this time I had seen only hazy images of her in my mind's eye, never a bodily apparition the way the first spirit had appeared. In my dream I was standing in my apartment, looking out at the view, when I heard her voice behind me. Turning, I saw the slinky form of Marilyn Monroe lounging on my new sofa, a glass of champagne in her hand.

"Don't look so surprised," the spirit said, laughing cattily. "Now let me tell you what to do to succeed in this town."

Then came my first instruction: I was to dye my hair platinum blond.

I awoke the next morning with that strange feeling that always follows too-real dreams. Rubbing my eyes, I threw my feet over the edge of the bed and stumbled into the bathroom. After flipping on the light, I stared at my reflection in the mirror and scowled. Marilyn was right. Nobody wanted to work with dirty blondes in this town. If I was going to be a star, I'd better start looking like one. Before jumping in the shower I rang up a local salon and made an appointment for that afternoon.

I was exhausted when I finally made it back to the apartment that evening, a bundle of packages in my arms. After getting my hair done, I'd squeezed in a little shopping time. New hair meant I had to have a new outfit or two. Somehow it had turned into five.

The new look was fabulous. My short, platinum coiffure framed a pretty face made even prettier with perfect make-up application. Men had always looked at me, but now they really stared—some even doing double takes.

I drew the blinds, turned on some New Age music and sat cross-legged on the living room floor to meditate. Emptying my mind, I allowed myself to drift into another level of consciousness. I had become adept at this and had even mastered the art of soul travel, leaving my body to visit some distant destination. Re-entry to my physical body was achieved through the shimmery gold cord I had first encountered as a child.

After about thirty minutes of meditation, I opened my eyes. There, sitting opposite me, lounging on the couch, was Marilyn—just as she had looked in my dream. She wore a champagne colored evening gown covered with bugle beads. She smiled languidly.

"Good girl," she said, nodding her approval.

From that time on, Marilyn was no longer just a voice. She appeared off and on throughout my days in a full-length, physical apparition that only I could see. She was my secret friend.

My success with "Country Top Twenty" didn't go unnoticed. Moving from one dance job to another, I quickly built a solid reputation as a professional. Doors opened for me to do commercials, and I won several big paying accounts that first year. As my reputation grew, I began to choreograph my own jobs, working with dancers, costume designers, and film directors. I received further training in acting at Actors Studio in Los Angeles and the American Conservatory Theatre in San Francisco, preparing for a transition into film.

I zig-zagged through the rush-hour traffic in my black Porsche and swung into a reserved parking space at the posh, three-story glass building. By now I was teaching a few classes a week at a prominent dance studio in West Hollywood. Grabbing my dance bag, I hurried inside and made my way to the second story room where my Jazz II class was already assembled. All the dancers were professionals, and their talk was sprinkled with tidbits of information on auditions for shows that were coming to town. There were no glitzy looks here. This was strictly a work environment. The hard lines of the dancers' faces—unsoftened by makeup at such an early hour—betrayed the grinding lifestyles they led. Most of them came to class with a cigarette in one hand and a steaming cup of coffee in the other. And no one tried to guess how many had already made a pit stop in the bathroom to snort a line of cocaine.

As I placed an album on the record player to start the warm-up, a girl ran in the door. *Another latecomer*, I thought to myself. But there was something very different about this girl. Covering her head was a shock of thick, purple hair. Stilling a snicker, I motioned to her to take a position in the back. Instead she moved right to the front, a friendly gleam in her eye.

Too overdone, I thought as I quickly assessed her appearance. She looked as if she'd walked straight off the set of *Flashdance.*

After class the bold, lilac-haired girl came up to me.

"Hi, my name's Jeri. That was a great class."

"Thanks," I said, wondering where this was going to lead.

But almost against my will I was drawn into easy conversation with Jeri. Noticing that the room had emptied, I glanced up at the clock. We'd been talking for twenty minutes.

"Listen, I have to get going, but I need to grab a bite to eat before a rehearsal this afternoon. Wanna join me?"

"Love to," Jeri said, picking up her leather dance bag and heading for the door. I smiled at her retreating figure. Something about this aggressive girl intrigued me. Over a dish of pasta later that hour, our friendship was solidified. Never before had I felt so at ease with a girl. From that day on we became fast friends. For the first time in my life I knew what it felt like to have a best friend—and I was twenty-three years old.

The years whizzed by. By the mid-1980s my life careened at a hectic pace, but it was a routine I found comforting. A typical day started around 7 a.m. I would get out of bed, grind up some coffee and meditate for twenty minutes.

After a quick shower, I'd rush to the dance studio where I assisted a prominent choreographer from 8:30 to 10:15 a.m. From then, it was ballet class until noon. After a bite of lunch, I'd give my commercial and theatrical agents a call to see if there were any auditions that day. If so, I would rush back to the apartment, check my phone messages, feed the cat, get dressed and race to the audition. If I was working on a long-term project, the balance of the afternoon was filled with rehearsals or actual shooting for commercials.

At night I attended acting and dance classes as well as taught a dance class. Whatever time was left over quickly filled up with dates and business appointments. Always watching my figure, I ate like a bird. Smoking a little pot helped me unwind every night as I collapsed on my living room sofa. Soon I graduated to cocaine.

Everything seemed to be going according to schedule. I had a great apartment, a fantastic friend, a sports car, and a cat.

Work, work, work. Marilyn was driving me, always propelling me deeper into Hollywood and its rat-race lifestyle. But this was what I had wanted, wasn't it? I shook back my hair and took a long drag on the marijuana joint in my hand, my eyes squinting through the smoke at the larger-than-life sign on the hill.

Chapter 9

Inside the New Age

*J*opened my eyes and strained to read the hands of the alarm clock on the bedside table. As I groped to shut off the offending alarm, I noticed the bloodstains on my pillow from the nosebleed of the night before.

"I've been working too hard and doing too much coke," I said out loud as I headed for the bathroom. It seemed as if one day were melting into the next.

It was 5:30 a.m. and in one hour I was expected on the set of a Mitsubishi commercial with all my mental faculties cranking. I had twelve dancers and an entire film crew waiting on me to come and choreograph this commercial. "Where's my purse?" I mumbled.

I found it on the floor. After rummaging around inside the purse, my hands closed on a small vial. I stooped over the sink and wet the inside of my nose to make it receptive to the cocaine. Flakes of dried blood fell onto the white porcelain as I snorted water into my nose. After locating the mirror I had used the night before, I carefully laid out three lines. The drug hit my system, and in a matter of seconds I was back in the game.

I pulled my leotards over my 110-pound frame, checked myself out in the mirror, kissed my cat, flipped on the telephone answering machine, and took off.

I had been staying at Jeri's apartment for a few weeks. That evening, as we slouched in the living room eating gourmet yogurt, the telephone rang.

"It's for you," Jeri said, looking puzzled. I was even more puzzled. I had not given anyone her number.

"Hello," I said hesitantly.

"Yes, hello. Is this Robin Harry?" a man's voice asked.

"Yes."

When the caller identified himself as Steven Baker, a prominent film and television director, goosebumps crawled up my arms.

"This is going to sound strange, but I need to find out who you are," he said, chuckling apologetically. "You see, when I came back from lunch today, your name and number were on my private list of people to call back. I have no earthly idea how they got there."

I told him I was a dancer and actress. He asked what work I had done, and from there the conversation flowed easily. When I finally hung up the phone twenty minutes later, I had an appointment to meet him at his office the next day.

As I drove through the manicured streets of Beverly Hills on my way to meet Mr. Baker, Marilyn spoke to my mind, detailing what would happen. She informed me that this was only a stepping stone to get me in with somebody big, somebody intricately connected.

I parked my Porsche in front of a sleek high-tech building. The number on the building was 666. Like most people, I had heard that this was the "number of the beast," whatever that meant, but it didn't alarm me in the slightest. After all, somebody had to have that address, right?

Minutes later I was sitting in the elegant office of Mr. Baker, chatting with him over a steaming cup of cappuccino.

"Why don't we do this over lunch instead," he suggested. "I know a great little Thai place."

"All right, but only if I drive," I said. I wanted to stay in control.

The maitre d' showed us to a private table in the garden section under a canopy of bamboo draped with greenery. Soft oriental music played in the background as we sipped our Thai iced tea. Gradually the conversation turned to our mutual belief, the New Age.

Mr. Baker asked a few more questions about my work, then he looked at me intently, his eyes piercing.

"I feel like this is a divine appointment. I've met people in my life who were destined to become stars. I see that in you."

He paused and twirled the miniature paper umbrella in his drink before continuing.

"There's a man I want you to meet. He hasn't taken on any new talent in about twenty-five years, and he's a very busy man. He may only give you two minutes, but something tells me I need to put you in touch with him. His name is Marvin Schlesser."

I recognized the name of the famous agent at once and almost shivered. He held a high position in a leading talent agency, and his influence was far-reaching. Everyone knew a rookie couldn't possibly get in with him.

"Why don't I arrange an appointment for you, say, tomorrow at ten o'clock?" Baker said. "If I tell him it's important, Marvin will squeeze you in."

At 9:45 the next morning, I found myself in the office of this highly connected man. I had given a lot of thought to my outfit: a beige suede tank top tucked into a white leather miniskirt, my smooth, golden-brown legs unspoiled by nylons. On my feet were white high-heeled pumps.

Marvin sat casually in a black and pink jogging suit, his designer glasses framing a face that had aged well, his black hair was peppered with gray, and a gold medallion dangled on his tanned upper chest. I guessed him to be in his mid-fifties. His office ruled almost one whole side of the building. A large picture window behind the desk provided a panorama of Beverly Hills, and the room was tastefully appointed with plush furnishings.

"So, Steve tells me you're somebody I ought to meet," he said, leaning back in his executive chair. "Tell me about yourself."

I knew I had only one shot at this, so I chose my words carefully, outlining for him my most promising work so far and leaving out the petty stuff. He listened, nodding his head now and then and asking a few questions. When I had finished, I glanced at my watch. It was 10:30. I had certainly made it past the two-minute zone.

By now Marvin was leaning forward, his arms folded across the desk in front of him. On his face was the same look I had seen on Steven Bakers the day before.

"Excuse me just a minute, please," he said. He picked up his telephone and buzzed his secretary.

"Charlotte, cancel all my appointments for the next

three hours. Yes, that's right. Thanks."

After hanging up the phone, he motioned me to take a seat on the cream-colored leather sofa at the far end of the office where a small sitting room had been created. He made me a drink, poured one for himself, then sat cross-legged on the floor. Adrenaline warmed my veins as I realized a connection had been made with this powerful man. It was more than chemistry. He seemed really interested in everything about me. What had my past been like? What were my dreams? My aspirations?

I talked on, eventually sharing about my spirituality. Encouraged by Marilyn, I grew bold enough to tell him I thought our meeting was "God." His eyes shined, and he nodded his head. He too believed in the power of the spirit. Marilyn appeared and disappeared several times during the three-hour meeting, sometimes sitting on the couch next to me, other times standing behind the chair that Marvin leaned against. At length he told me he was prepared to represent me professionally. By that time I was not even surprised. I glanced up over his head. Marilyn smiled her sultry smile, her red lips parting slightly. Everything grew quiet. Only the bubbling of the aquarium broke the still-ness. Marvin glanced around the room then fastened his eyes on mine.

"Do you have a spirit guide?" he said softly.

"Yes," I said, watching for his reaction.

"Is it Marilyn Monroe?"

His discernment startled me. "Yes," I half-whispered, my voice husky.

"Is she here now?"

I nodded.

Marvin's eyes gleamed. "I used to do some work for her when she was alive."

My heart thumped wildly as I stepped into the elevator an hour later. On the drive home I thought how lucky I was to have Marilyn on my side. Clearly, the last two days had been arranged by her. By now I was convinced that my imminent stardom would become a platform for me to share my enlightenment with the world. The quantum leap, the one-world religion, spirituality. These were all themes of my vision for the future. During hours of meditation, Marilyn had shared these concepts with me. Now I knew, Marvin was the man with the connections.

A few days later my tarot card reader, Sam, invited me to a private meeting of psychics in Mill Valley, a New Age mecca located in Northern California. I had been attending these types of meetings on a regular basis, learning all I could about the New Age. This particular meeting was hosted by a Mrs. Langley, a very powerful woman in the movement who had written numerous books on the subject. Her guest was to be a well-known medium, or channeler, a person who allows spirits to speak through him or her.

The air grew cool, though the sun was bright, as my Porsche wound its way up the mountain and finally turned in at the driveway of a cedar house built right on the mountainside. Several other luxury cars were already there.

After cocktails and introductions, the twenty or so guests were asked to be seated. I recognized a few people from other meetings I had attended and selected a place on the sprawling sectional sofa next to a woman who looked familiar.

The medium's assistant walked into the spacious room. Taking no time for pleasantries, she led us into a meditative state. The atmosphere was almost crackling with psychic energy by the time the medium walked in, escorted by Mrs. Langley. She sat down in the chair placed at the front for her.

Her bland housewife appearance belied her power in the spirit realm. She looked as if she could be anyone's next-door neighbor.

"Now she is going to channel the descended master," the assistant said.

As the medium opened her mouth and spoke, a wave of nausea washed over me, and I felt rooted to my seat. The voice that emanated from her mouth was deep and masculine. It spoke in a commanding monotone, expounding on spiritual things and teaching us how to become more one with the universe—more one with "God." I couldn't take my eyes off the medium as the presence of the spirit she was channeling filled the room. I had witnessed numerous channelings, but this one frightened me.

When the voice ended, the medium looked directly at me, got up and walked from the room. Gradually the spell was broken, and quiet small talk resumed among the guests. I headed to the refreshment table to refill my drink; I needed something to calm my rattled nerves. Someone tapped me on the shoulder. It was the medium's assistant.

"The spirit wants to speak to you," she said, her face expressionless. It was more of a command than an invitation. She motioned me to follow her.

The assistant led me through a side door that opened onto a garden filled with tropical trees and brightly colored flowers. A stone path that cut through the middle of the garden led to a small, star-shaped building set off from the main house. Built of redwood planks inset with stained-glass windows, this was a star chamber, an ashram, a meditative center. I had heard of these mystical chambers before but had never actually seen one.

As I entered the star room, the sickening sensation gripped me again. The room was filled with bright light. I looked up to see where it was coming from. The entire ceiling of the building was glass, and the sun was at its zenith. Mrs. Langley and the channeler were sitting there waiting for me.

"Come in and sit down," Mrs. Langley said.

I complied like an obedient child.

"Now, darling, we have brought you here for a very specific purpose," she continued.

I could feel the medium's eyes boring into me like red-hot pokers. She frightened me.

"You are here at the request of the spirit," Mrs. Langley was saying.

"You will lead people," the masculine voice cut in.

I looked at the woman, not knowing what to think.

She reached over and gripped my hands in hers.

"You will become famous. You have already connected with the man. He will help you. Soon you will meet the woman, the famous woman who knows. She will be like a mother to you. You will walk in her footsteps."

The voice continued, describing in remarkable detail my past and my present and prophesying my future.

As I left the house that day, Mrs. Langley hugged me and told me that if I needed anything, she would supply it.

"We take care of our own," she said.

She handed me an envelope. In it was a card printed with the date and time of the next meeting.

A week later my new boyfriend and I were relaxing at my apartment. I was deep in thought about my encounter with the medium.

"What's wrong with you, Robin?" Brian asked.

"You've been acting strange lately." I looked up and read serious concern on his face. Brian and I had been dating for three months. A drummer for a popular rock band, he had seen me at a chic Hollywood party and made his way over to talk to me. We had hit it off right from the start. I loved everything about him—his sweet personality, his glitzy life-style, his gorgeous looks. Brian had chiseled features and thick black hair that just touched his shoulders.

"Oh, nothing," I said. "I was just thinking."

"About what?"

"It's that psychic meeting I went to last week. Ever since then I haven't been able to shake off the creepy-crawlies."

Brian stared at me for a moment, "Robin, what happened to you up there? What did those people do to you? Sometimes I get weird vibes when I'm around you. I never used to feel that before." For explanation, I walked over to the kitchen table and pulled a cassette out of my purse. It was a tape recording of the channeler's prophecy over me in the star room. For some reason I carried it with me everywhere.

Brian listened to the tape, then shut the cassette recorder off. He breathed out slowly. I realized he had been holding his breath.

"Sweetheart, this is weird stuff. I've been in rock and roll a long time. I've seen a lot of satanic stuff, and this is creepy. What do you want with this sort of thing?"

"No, Brian," I countered. "This is just one example of higher revelation in the New Age. Spirit guides are here to help us. Didn't you hear what the prophecy said? I'm going to be famous."

"And that room you told me about," Brian said, ignoring my words, "that star chamber. Do you know what it means?"

"Well...no, not really."

"A five-pointed star is a pentagram, Robin. The pentagram is a satanic symbol."

"Oh, come on, Brian," I said. "The star shape is just a coincidence. There are stars everywhere. Don't worry about me. I'll be fine."

But later that night, alone with my thoughts, I knew that I was not alright. Ever since that meeting at Mrs. Langley's, I had been tormented in my dreams. Sometimes I sensed I was being pursued by something—just as that horrible spirit had stalked me at college. Worse, I had begun to catch glimmers of a hostile side to Marilyn's nature. At times now she grew argumentative, snapping at me if I didn't jump to do her bidding.

"I want you to wear this dress to your audition today," she said one morning, gesturing to a particular outfit in my closet.

But I had been asserting my own mind lately and refused her choice, even though I knew it was the better one.

"I said this dress," Marilyn reiterated.

"I heard what you said, but I'm going to choose my own clothes today, thank you." I yanked another dress off its hanger.

"Go ahead, sweetheart," she said viciously. "But you won't get the audition." She was right. I didn't.

The next time I was a little more obedient to appease my fickle guiding spirit. I needed her help to keep achieving, and we both knew it. Our relationship became strained, teetering back and forth between positive, which meant I always obeyed her commands, and not-so-positive, those times when I disobeyed her.

A few nights later Brian came over again. I had promised to cook him a gourmet supper. After dinner we sipped glasses of Dom Pérignon champagne as we relaxed on the sofa. Soft music played in the background. Candlelight flickered on the walls. The mood was perfect. Brian leaned over and kissed me passionately.

Suddenly he pulled back, his eyes full of fright. "Oh, my God!"

He stood up, walked over to the wall and turned on the light switch. After a minute he came back to the sofa, taking a seat at the far end. He was shaking.

"What is it?" I asked. But already I sensed his answer. At the moment he kissed me, I had felt my spirit guide enter me. It was a forcible entry, as if she had wanted to kiss Brian through me.

"What's wrong, Brian?" I said.

"Oh, my God," he said again, rubbing his hands over his eyes. "This is too weird."

"*What?*"

He looked up at me. "I wasn't kissing you, Robin. It wasn't you."

"What do you mean? What did you see?"

"I saw Marilyn Monroe. It wasn't your face, Robin. It wasn't you."

Visibly shaken, Brian made an excuse and left my apartment. I was furious with Marilyn. She had invaded me, used me without permission. I shouted angry insults and threats to her, but she had vanished for the night.

Over the next few months I continued to attend meetings with Mrs. Langley's crowd. I could hardly do otherwise; they were so insistent. Always there was a phone message or a note in the mail about this or that upcoming get together. My presence was expected. I went along, allowing them to think I was ready to move up to the next rung in the New Age ladder. But instinctively I pulled back, sensing an emerging evil in their midst. Meanwhile a battle raged in my mind. It was becoming uncomfortably clear that Marilyn and I were in a power struggle for my mind—and my soul. I was determined not to let her win.

Chapter 10

The Accident

The time was 6 p.m. I had already put in a ten-hour day on the set of a Coca-Cola commercial; now I had to rush to Beverly Hills where I was working part-time as a waitress in a hip Italian restaurant on La Cienega Boulevard. Most people didn't think I needed to work this job, but a dancer's income is not always steady. Besides, I wanted to pay off my Porsche. Shifting the car into third gear, I passed a slow-moving Pontiac full of shutterbugs.

"Stupid tourists," I muttered as I flew past. "Haven't you ever seen a palm tree before?"

After screeching to a halt at the restaurant, I hurried in the back entrance.

"Hey, baby!"

It was Tony, the sleazy manager who thought he was Fonzy. As usual, he was dressed in black pants and a loud silk shirt. Three or four gold chains flittered on his hairy upper chest.

"You're late."

Whoever made this idiot a manager? I thought as I tugged

open the closet door next to the bar to stash my purse. The nine-foot-high utility closet was built into the wall some three feet off the floor and was actually part of the wall. It was made of solid oak about six inches thick and was covered with bamboo on the outside to blend in with the rest of the wall. I always opened it carefully, because the hinges were loose.

"I was working on a commercial, ok? I'm sorry," I said, then reached behind the bar for my apron.

"What are you, a movie star or a waitress?" came the retort.

"That's a good question," I shot back as I headed for the kitchen.

The posh restaurant was a hangout for stars and entertainment people. You couldn't get a meal there for under a hundred dollars per couple. I could earn two hundred dollars a weekend in tips and still make auditions, do commercials and other television work, and teach dance during the week.

Most of the girls who worked there were struggling actresses waiting for their big break. They were all pretty. In L.A. pretty faces and sparkling personalities are a dime a dozen. My best friend, Jeri, had gotten a job there as well. She waved to me as I walked into the kitchen. By now her hair was back to its natural color, a rich reddish-brown that fell in thick wavy locks around her pretty face. We chatted with each other as the restaurant filled up on that May evening of 1985.

"Did you see Tony?" she asked.

"Yeah," I said. "It's going to be one of those nights."

"Sometimes I hate that creep."

"What do you mean, sometimes?" I said, giggling.

"Hey, Jeri, you know what?"

"What?" she said, her green eyes suddenly serious at the tone in my voice.

"You know," I said, holding her attention, "my life has consisted of a chain of abusive relationships resulting from a deep sense of doubt and insecurity."

"What?" she laughed. "What are you talking about?"

I put on my most serious face, knowing that at any moment I might laugh.

"At least that's what my shrink said yesterday."

"Shut up, you weird chick," she said, and we both burst into fits of laughter. Jeri and I were always kidding around with each other. It felt good to have a buddy.

"Look who just walked in," a fellow waitress said as she pushed past me. "Looks like they're in your section."

The hostess was escorting two VIPs to a corner booth where Tony was sitting. One man was a very influential director and the other was the star of a popular nighttime television series. Everyone in the place turned and looked as they were seated. The two men received their audience with ease, as if the attention was expected.

Someday everyone will do that for me, I thought as I slipped off into a daydream.

"Hey, Robin, wake up!" Jeri said as she passed by her arms filled with plates of steaming pasta.

This was the type of restaurant where people came to be seen. Beautifully decorated in orchids and grays, the main dining room was open and airy, surrounded by windows that reached to the vaulted ceiling. A profusion of greenery and polished brass warmed the atmosphere. Guests were served at glass-top tables by pretty waitresses wearing tight white pants, crisp white shirts, a khaki tie, and matching apron.

The celebrity watched me as I approached his table. He nudged the director next to him, who was talking on his cellular telephone. The celebrity whispered something to Tony and they all chuckled. "If it isn't the movie star," Tony teased. All three men took a long, sweeping look at me. I felt violated, as if I were standing there naked. Blood rushed to my face, creating a pink flush that I desperately hoped would go unnoticed. "I will not let them intimidate me," I said to myself. In Hollywood the rule of survival is intimidate or be intimidated.

"Can I get you something to drink before dinner?" I asked in my most professional voice. I set my jaw and prepared to take their order.

"I hear you did a Coca-Cola commercial today," the director said. "How'd it go?"

"Great," I said. "It turned out wonderful."

"I heard that you're a professional dancer," the celebrity said. "Is it true what they say about dancers?"

I felt anger rising within me. He laughed and looked at his table mates for support. They all stared at me, waiting for a reaction.

"Can I get you something to drink before dinner?" I asked again.

Somewhat deflated, they gave me their orders, and I quickly escaped to the safety of the bathroom. After making sure I was alone, I pulled a tiny vial from my apron and took a couple of hits of cocaine.

"Thank God for drugs," I said aloud as new strength shot

through me.

Grabbing my order pad, I hurried to the bar to place the drink order. The bar was situated in the front of the restaurant near the guest desk. Seeing the hostess standing there, I asked her to take the drinks to the table for me.

"I'm not going over to that table until I cool off," I told her. The bartender overheard and nodded in agreement as he started to fill the order. Also an actor, he was familiar with the power trips some celebrities play.

Relieved of my burden, I went into the kitchen and leaned against the wall. Suddenly a compulsion seized me, and I heard an inner voice say, "You can't let them get to you like that! If you let them do it now, they will always have the upper hand. Go out there and take that drink order!" It was a command that was accompanied by an invisible push toward the bar. I responded immediately and rushed back through the double swinging doors to the bar area. I spotted the hostess, drink tray in hand. She was just about to take the drinks to the table.

"Wait!" I said. "Let me take those."

The hostess looked up, startled, as I grabbed the tray from her hand. Involuntarily she took two or three steps back, a look of alarm on her face. "Look out!" someone shouted too late.

A split second later the 150-pound door to the utility closet behind me fell out of the wall and came crashing down on me. I screamed as it struck my skull. As I crumpled to the floor, the door followed me down and landed directly on top of me.

"Get that door off her!" somebody yelled. I could hear hushed voices all around me but could barely make out what they were saying. I caught the end of someone saying, "Get her out of here before anyone notices!"

Then Tony's voice rose loud and clear above the rest. "Don't use an ambulance. It will attract too much attention. Just get her to a hospital."

The door was hoisted off me. The last thing I remembered before blackness closed in was being carried out to the backseat of a car.

Chapter 11

Sterile Walls, Shattered Dreams

*J*opened my eyes and looked over to my right. Jeri was sitting there, her face lined with worry. Something was wrong. *My bedroom walls aren't white,* I thought as I struggled to place the room. The blinds of the window were pulled shut, so I couldn't tell if it was night or day.

"Jeri," I said, reaching out for her hand.

My arm stopped short as I felt something pull at my wrist. I looked down and saw several IVs hooked to my pale arm.

"God, where am I?" I said shakily "I can't feel my body."

I tried to talk to Jeri, but the words came out as if in slow motion. I could hear myself, but I wasn't making any sense. Suddenly I started to shake violently.

"Help! Somebody help!" Jeri shouted as she reached for something at the side of my bed.

"Don't worry. Hold on, Robin. The nurse is coming," she said, but I saw fear in her eyes.

She held my hand and watched the door as if she had done this many times before. The door opened and a nurse rushed in with a hypodermic needle in her hand. She yanked the bedsheet off me and turned me on my side.

"What's this?" I tried to say. Wait, wait, what's going on here?" No one seemed to understand what I was saying.

Jeri took control of the situation, helping the nurse by holding me still.

In moments the pain and shaking stopped. The nurse stood over me and placed her hand on my shoulder. I stared, frightened and confused, at my friend, my eyes pleading for explanation and reassurance.

"Don't try to talk," Jeri said, smoothing my brow. "Just rest."

I slipped into a deep, coma-like sleep. Inside that dark, safe place my mind struggled to put the pieces of the puzzle together.

A few days later I awakened to find someone standing beside my bed. The stranger was a small man with tortoise-shell spectacles and dark, wavy hair. He was scribbling something on a clipboard, his face intent. A few moments passed before he looked up.

"Ah, good, you're awake," he said. "I'm Dr. Sellerman. I'll be your physician while you're here at Cedars-Sinai Medical Center. How are you feeling today?"

"Fine," I lied.

"Miss Harry, your condition is what we call post-concussive syndrome, which means impaired functioning of the brain as a result of a blow to the head. You've suffered major damage to your motor control center. That's why you're having trouble moving your arms and legs. At the point of impact, your muscles also tensed into spasms. Those spasms are creating the frequent seizures you're experiencing. We're running some more tests, and I've got a specialist in neuro-surgery coming in tomorrow to check you over. But as far as we can tell, the main thing we're dealing with is controlling the spasms. The only treatment we've found effective is large doses of Demerol."

"When will I be well?" I asked bluntly.

The doctor was thoughtful a moment, then said, "Let's take it one day at a time. As soon as you're strong enough we'll move you to rehab."

The days passed with one uncontrollable seizure follow-ing another, each one remedied by a shot of Demerol or morphine. Each time I slipped back into sleep, only to be awakened by the next attack. Whenever I was awake, Jeri brought me up to date on who had called and who had sent flowers. A big bouquet from Mom and Dad sat on the bedside table. At my request, Jeri had telephoned my parents and deliberately downplayed the seriousness of my condition. She told them I was being treated for a concus-sion, but that everything was fine. There was no need for them to rush down from Vallejo. The truth was, I wasn't ready to see them. Resentment over their leaving me at the ranch for so long had festered within me through the years, and now I wasn't sure how I felt about them. Holding them at bay was the easiest way to deal with it.

During the weeks that followed, as I drifted in and out of drug-induced sleep, I searched for an answer. In my waking hours and in my dreaming hours I had one continual thought, *Why had the accident happened to me?* As a fervent New Ager, I believed everything happened for a reason. What was the purpose behind this? I called out to my spirit guide for explanation, but she was nowhere to be found. In my time of worst need, Marilyn seemed to have abandoned me. That once-insistent inner voice was now silent.

Vivid dreams haunted my unconscious hours, sometimes frightening, sometimes bittersweet as I saw scenes of my life played out on a huge screen in my feverish mind. I saw myself as a baby, a shy little girl, a determined young woman striving to beat the odds stacked against her. As I watched this surreal movie in my dreams, a strange thing started to happen. From as far back as I could remember, I had been very hard on myself, always striving to achieve. Now, as I relived the major events of my life, I was filled with compassion for that little girl, that determined young woman, even the woman I had become. Often, when I woke from these dreams, my cheeks were wet with tears.

Day after day, night after night, I fought the pain and violent shaking that seized my body. Sometimes I would manage to stay awake a few hours, staring vacantly at the white, sanitized walls of my hospital room or watching the flowers from friends wilt before my eyes, one petal at a time.

My life became dream-like. I looked down and saw thin arms with ugly, purple bruises surrounding the needle that was fastened there. The IV had to be moved continually as vein after vein collapsed from overuse. Was this sallow, bony frame my body? What had happened to my graceful dancer's form? I gradually learned to welcome the long periods of unconsciousness. Realty had become such a horror.

"Have you tried to meditate?" I heard Jeri say from my bedside one morning.

I hadn't even realized she was still there. It seemed as if she had been there a long time.

"I'm afraid to," I said groggily, remembering the last inner voice I had heard. "Last time I tried, I just felt confusion. I'm not sure what's going on. I can't seem to get my mind clear."

"But Marilyn could help you through this time," Jeri said.

I closed my eyes and collected my thoughts before trying to explain.

"Jeri," I said, "I heard a voice the night I got hurt, and it told me to take that drink tray. That's when the door came down and hit me. It doesn't make sense. There were enough people standing around that someone should've been able to warn me in time. I mean, when a door like that falls off its hinges, it falls like a tree, right? There should have been at least a few seconds. Jeri, that thing hit me too hard and too fast to have been normal."

Jeri looked at me in astonishment. "You don't think Marilyn would do that, do you?"

I shrugged. "Why had those unseen hands compelled me to go to the bar at that very moment, as if the stage were set and all that remained was to get the main character, me, in position before the cue was given to drop the door?"

"Maybe it wasn't Marilyn's voice," I sighed, "but where is she?"

Four weeks had passed since the accident, I was told. Even though the blinds were shut, I knew it was morning because *Tom and Jerry* was on TV. The story of cat gets mouse. *Not unlike the entertainment business*, I thought wryly.

I looked up and saw Dr. Sellerman coming through the door. "Time to go," he said with a smile.

I was finally ready to be moved to a rehabilitation unit. There was a sense of excitement in the air as the orderlies lifted me off the bed and placed me in my new mode of transportation, a wheelchair. I was so weak my head drooped down on my chest.

Dr. Sellerman looked down at me and said, "Are you ready, Robin?"

I lifted my head and smiled feebly. "Let's go," I said, believing in my heart that I was on my way to total recovery.

Out of the room we went, down hospital corridors, out onto the sidewalk, and into a whole new building, the Shuman Rehabilitation Clinic.

"You don't know how fortunate you are to be going here," Dr. Sellerman said as he walked along beside my wheelchair. "They accept only thirty cases at a time. I had to go before a review board to get you in, but if anyone can make you walk again, they can."

We got to the elevator and started our way up to the sixth floor. As the elevator door opened, my heart sank. Sitting there waiting to use the elevator were six or seven patients with nurses by their sides. Some patients were strapped into their wheelchairs. Some had no arms; others had no legs. Some were partially or totally paralyzed; others had shaved heads from where brain tumors had been removed. It looked like a convoy returning home from Vietnam on medical discharge.

They sat smiling bravely, dealing with the cruel blow life had dealt them. My stomach churned.

I don't belong here. I'm not that bad....

My train of thought was interrupted by Dr. Sellerman's voice.

"Don't let them scare you," he whispered as he pushed me past, sensing the panic rising within me.

"These are desperate cases," I said. "What am I doing here?"

Dr. Sellerman looked at me with eyes of compassion.

"The therapists here are the best, Robin. They can make you walk again."

The orderly wheeled me into my room, where I got my first glimpse of my new roommate sitting there in her wheelchair, head shaved, face bloated from radiation therapy.

"I'm Christy," she said.

I found out later that Christy was a thirty-two year-old attorney who had a cancerous brain tumor. When the doctors removed it, she was left paralyzed from the neck down. Dr. Sellerman mentioned that she needed cheering up and was hoping I could be a friend to her. She had lost everything but her life and now passed the days in a listless state of depression.

Dr. Sellerman left to attend to his other patients, and I looked around the walls of my new home, almost ready to cry.

At that moment Jeri, my faithful friend, walked through the door carrying an enormous balloon bouquet. Stuffed in her pockets were candy bars for me. Even though I still couldn't hold down food, I could munch on an occasional chocolate bar.

We're on our way to recovery," she said as she plopped down on the bed.

"This place is a trip," I said with a half-smile."Oh, Jeri, this is Christy; Christy, this is my best friend, Jeri." The two exchanged polite greetings.

Jeri surveyed our new territory with feigned intensity,

then pronounced, "Well, it looks just like a hospital to me."

We had a good laugh together. Jeri always made me laugh. She came every day with the same tireless exuberance to help me through and keep me going. She had quit her job at the restaurant shortly after my accident. The management never inquired after my condition or my progress. It was as if I had dropped off the face of the earth. My world became a hospital room, a wheelchair, visits from Jeri, and hours of pain and seizures.

"Here are your new glasses," she said, handing me a pair of prescription glasses that had been ordered for me. I had lost 80 percent of my peripheral vision because of the blow to my head.

"Great," I said blandly, putting the frames on and making a funny face at Jeri.

Rehab started at 9 a.m. each morning. After I woke, the nurse gave me pain medication, then I was shuttled off to rehab classes, one after another—speech therapy, physical therapy, occupational therapy and biofeedback therapy. I would finish by four o'clock in the afternoon. Jeri usually came bouncing in around 4:30 and kept me company until visiting hours were over.

One day as I was wheeled back into my room, I saw a familiar, handsome face. It was Brian. The last time he had seen me I was a beautiful, sleek bodied dancer. Now I was only a shell of the woman I had been. Several times while I was in ICU he had left telephone messages. I had never returned them, thinking it best if Brian just forgot about me.

Inadvertently I dropped my eyes to my lap. Shame at my appearance and the fear of rejection washed over me. Here I was, a rising starlet whose light had fizzled out. Dark roots muddied my platinum blond hair, and my skin was pale and blotchy from all the pain medication.

"Hey, baby," Brian said, his gentle brown eyes glowing. "Why didn't you ever return my calls? I was half out of my mind when they told me what happened, but I couldn't get away from the tour. I just got back a couple of hours ago." I smiled in spite of myself. He still cared about me.

"Come here, you," I said, throwing my arms open wide. Brian stooped to hug me tight.

Over the next month Brian became a regular visitor, squeezing in time to see me between band rehearsals and out-of-town trips. He and Jeri were my link to sanity.

With the physical exertion of therapy, I now consumed even more pain medication than before and quickly became addicted. I took three different pain pills every four hours. Even though nearly two months had passed since the accident, I was still having four to five seizures a day. My whole body would shake violently for half an hour, the only remedy being a shot of potent medication. My therapists hoped to teach me through biofeedback to control the seizures without the aid of drugs.

"It's time for me to go home," Christy said one afternoon, her face averted.

"What? I can't hear you from over here," I said. "Hold on."

I wheeled over from the window to Christy's bed, where she was sitting.

"I'm going home tomorrow. I guess this is good-bye."

"But you're not completely better, Christy. They can't discharge you until you're well," I said indignantly.

"They took me into a meeting today with all my doctors

and therapists and told me they had done all that can be done. I'm going home." I stared at her, dumfounded and secretly horror-stricken. *But what will she do?* I wondered looking at her useless limbs and bloated body.

"Don't worry, I can at least get around," Christy said, reading my mind.

"You're going to do great," I responded, summoning up a bright smile. "You're going to be just fine."

All that night I thought about Christy and how she would make her way in the outside world. A hollow feeling in the pit of my stomach finally found words of expression in my mind: *Would I ever be normal again?*

The very next day Dr. Sellerman walked through the door with his usual springy step.

After poking and prodding me in doctoral fashion, he said, "I want you to stay in and rest today."

"Why? What's wrong?"

"Well, I want to do some more brain scans and some more testing. I'd like you to be rested up first."

The motor ability in my brain was impaired by the accident, and the doctors were attempting to re-educate my muscles to connect with my brain's commands.

I sighed and nodded in the manner of one resigned to whatever fate kicked her way.

Almost as soon as Dr. Sellerman disappeared, I heard the jingle of car keys coming down the hall. I looked up and saw my theatrical agent, Marvin Schlesser, poking his head in the door.

"How's my girl?" he said, setting down his ever present cellular telephone and the keys to his Jaguar.

"Hey, I haven't seen you for a while," I teased. "I thought

you forgot about your up-and-coming star." Since the accident I hadn't seen Marvin at all, although he had phoned a few times.

From our first meeting Marvin and I had sensed a mutual connection. I smiled as he talked on, bringing me up to date with Tinsel Town news.

"Say, listen, when do you think you're going to get out of here?" he asked.

"I don't know. Right now I'm really not sure what's going to happen. How's business?"

"Everything's great. I just got back from Las Vegas. Listen, I just stopped by to say hello. I gotta run. If you need anything, call Charlotte at my office. I love you, baby."

Marvin leaned down and kissed me on the cheek. "Keep your chin up," he said, then disappeared through the door.

As he left my room, I knew Marvin realized that my career was over.

Chapter 12

Baby Steps

D
r. Sellerman walked briskly into my room and opened the blinds, spilling the hot June sunlight into the sterile atmosphere. He turned to me with a big smile on his face.

"Tomorrow your therapists are going to get you up to try to walk," he pronounced.

I stared at him in silence. This was the moment I'd been waiting for. Yet suddenly I found myself panicking. *What if I can't do it?*

"That's great," I said finally, returning his smile. He sensed my hesitation.

"Don't worry, Robin, you'll do fine," he said, squeezing my hand.

I had been learning how to use my fingers again, how to transfer from a wheelchair to the shower, how to set up a kitchen for use from a wheelchair, how to dress myself and all the other basic functions an able-bodied person takes for granted. I secretly called it survival training for a cripple. In my therapy I had also tackled numerous puzzles, played computer games to re-educate my mind and heaved my way through physical exercises to strengthen my body.

Now they were going to make me walk again. That evening I went to sleep with quiet expectation. Around 2 a.m. I was jerked out of sleep by a violent seizure. I gripped the side of the bed for support and screamed out for the nurse. Somehow I found the call button and pushed it. My entire body wrenched uncontrollably as darts of white hot pain shot through me. Something added to my fear: lately I had the uneasy feeling that something dark and heavy was pressing down on me, intensifying the seizures.

The night nurse ran in with a hypodermic needle and injected tranquilizers into my system. Within moments I sagged limp in my bed. Gradually sleep returned in slow, painful waves.

Morning came, and with it Dr. Sellerman's quick step in the corridor. I looked up at him weakly as he came through the door.

"Had a rough couple of days, huh?" The seizures had hit hard, one right after another, for the past few days and nights.

I nodded.

He automatically started poking and prodding me. I jerked away from each touch, wincing in pain.

"How are you feeling now?"

He started the examination all over again, this time holding me securely.

I looked at him, trying to think of the right description: "I feel as if I've been run over by a speeding train, chewed up by a starving tiger, and thrown off a cliff with only jagged rocks to break my fall."

"Oh, is that all," he said, grinning. "It could be worse. We could have called off your walk today."

"Dr. Sellerman, you mean I do get to walk today?"

"That depends on you," he said. "Everything is set up at rehab."

He helped me sit up so he could finish the examination, then he took out a medical kit with needles in it and injected several tiny needles directly into my muscles. It hurt.

"I want to walk today," I said resolutely.

I looked over at the empty bed where my roommate had been and wondered when I would ever get out of this place and what condition I would leave it in.

"You about ready to get out of here?" he asked, as if reading my thoughts.

I stared blankly ahead, not knowing what to say. He injected nine more shots into my back. "Dr. Sellerman, how am I going to be when you finally release me? Am I still going to be a cripple?"

He carefully put away the needles in the medical bag before answering me.

"Robin," he said as he turned to face me, "we are doing everything in our power to make you as good as new; you have my word on that."

A *perfect non-answer*, I thought as he waved at me and walked out to make his rounds.

The hospital aide came to fetch me at 9 a.m. He brought in my wheelchair and extended his arm to help.

"I'll do it myself, if it's all right with you," I said as I maneuvered myself from the bed to the wheelchair.

"And away we go," he said.

I had eaten a good breakfast, brushed my own teeth, combed my own hair, and put myself in my own wheelchair. I was ready to walk.

I arrived at the rehab session ready to go. The physical therapists fastened weights to my legs and a weight belt around my waist. I looked as if I were getting outfitted for a moon walk. The weights were to help me feel my legs, which would help my muscles make a connection with the impaired motor center in my brain.

With a therapist on each side and one in front, they stood me up, holding me underneath the arms. The room was crowded with other patients working in their designated therapy stations. I tried to move my legs, and immediately my whole body started to quiver.

"It's ok. Keep trying," I heard someone say.

The therapists moved my feet forward, then told me to look at my legs and concentrate. I did. Slowly and painfully I inched forward. Suddenly the room exploded with cheers and wild clapping. I had an audience. Now I tried even harder.

"Go get Dr. Sellerman!" someone yelled excitedly.

Moments later he ran into the room.

"I knew you could do it! I just knew you could!" he said, his eyes shining.

He watched as three therapists helped me and I took my first steps, just as if I were a child starting all over again.

"I did it," I said to my proud doctor. "I really did it." Only then did I realize tears were streaming down my face.

All the other patients stared at me, glimmers of hope on their faces, as I was wheeled out of rehab and back to my room. "Today is a great day," I told the attendant as he steered me down the corridor. My eyes filled again as I realized there might be hope after all.

Later that day, still floating on cloud nine, I stared up at the ceiling trying to get myself into a meditative state. I couldn't seem to reach my guiding spirit.

"Marilyn," I said aloud, "Marilyn, where are you?"

Maybe she was mad at me for not trusting her. Maybe she thought I secretly accused her of trying to hurt me— even kill me.

Jeri came prancing through the door.

"Hey, champ, I heard the news. The whole hospital is buzzing. You walked today!" She tried to give me a big hug without inflicting pain and ended up just squeezing me softly.

"Your mom and dad are coming today," she said "Are you ready?"

I nodded and smiled. But I was nervous about seeing my mother especially. Things had been tense between us for several years. During my climb to further my career, I had become extremely selfish and shut her out completely. Deep inside I had wanted to punish her for abandoning me for six years of my childhood. But lying flat on my back had given me a lot of time to reflect. She was my *mother*; I knew I had some making up to do.

"Are you nervous?" Jeri asked as she took out my blue silk pajamas.

I felt tears spring to my eyes.

"I don't want them to be upset when they see me," I lied. "I don't look too great." That was true enough, I told myself, thinking about the weight I had lost, the dark circles under my eyes and the fact that I shook slightly.

A soft knock interrupted my thoughts. The door opened, and there was my mom, her arms full of flowers, my dad following close behind. I was sitting in my wheelchair dressed in my best pajamas and wearing the bravest look I could muster.

"Baby," she whispered in a rush of emotion as she ran over to me and held me tenderly. There were tears in her eyes.

"I didn't know it was this bad," she said. My father bent down and kissed me. Mom started pulling assorted things out of the bags Dad was carrying.

"I thought you might need these," she said. Finally she pulled out a blue velvet box.

"This is just because," she said, handing it to me.

I opened the box and looked down at the diamond watch that lay cradled inside.

"Oh, Mom, I love it," I said. "And I love you both very much." At that moment I realized all would be forgiven between us. I had my mother back again.

Suddenly I noticed Dr. Sellerman leaning quietly against the door.

"I thought you'd left for the day," I said. He never stayed this late unless there was some kind of emergency.

"I wanted to show your mother and father how you can walk so I stayed a little late. Do you mind?" He introduced himself to my parents, shook my father's hand and helped me to my feet. I took about eight or nine steps, just a few inches each, shaking slightly and leaning heavily on Dr. Sellerman's arm.

"Isn't she great?" he said, beaming at my parents.

My mom and dad nodded mutely, grasping for the first

time the seriousness of my condition. As I sat down in my wheelchair, I could see a mixture of joy and deep sadness cross their faces.

A seizure hit. Dr. Sellerman rang for the nurse and asked everyone to leave the room.

"Please, doctor, let me stay," Mom pleaded.

The nurse ran in with the shot, helped Dr. Sellerman lift me onto the bed and injected the needle into my hip. I looked up and saw my mom watching helplessly as her youngest daughter shook uncontrollably.

I loved her more at that moment than I ever had in my whole life. She moved forward and held my hand. I could hear her whisper, "It's gonna be all right, baby. Mama's here."

I slipped into another drug induced sleep and remained unconscious for the next several hours. As I slept, I began to dream, wandering directionless through my subconscious mind. I found myself in a log cabin somewhere deep in the woods. It was damp and dark and cold. I had been here before.

Yes, there across the room was the rock fireplace. I walked over to the open window. Along a narrow woodland path galloped a white horse. It was heading straight for the cabin. On its back was a woman wearing a long, dark blue dress and a cloak. She had the coldest steel-blue eyes I had ever seen—eyes that seemed to beckon me against my will....

"No! No! No!" I screamed out, trying to wake myself up. "This is only a dream. You're not real."

I felt claw-tipped fingers grip my arms and push me through the door.

"Let me go," I sobbed. "Let me go."

"What's wrong, child?" said a voice over me. Instantly I snapped back into the waking world. It was Thelma, the sweet nurse who reminded me of Scarlett O'Hara's mammy.

She was holding me tightly. I looked around. Gradually calm replaced frenzy as I recognized the white, sterile walls of my hospital room. Thelma had heard me screaming and rushed into my room to wake me.

"She wants to take me away," I stammered.

"Who wants to take you, sweetie?"

"The witch," I blurted. "My mom told me she's a witch."

Thelma looked at me long and hard.

"Don't you understand?" I said. "I'm like her!"

"Child, now I'm a prayin' woman. Don't you start none of this nonsense with me."

"You don't understand," I screamed in hysteria as another seizure took me in its grip.

Thelma ran out of the room and returned moments later.

"Roll over," she commanded, then injected drugs into my shaking body. I saw her mumbling something under her breath as I slipped into darkness. It sounded like a prayer.

Chapter 13

Homecoming

The early morning commotion of the hospital awakened me. Someone had already opened my blinds, and rays of light crept into my room, playing shadow games on the walls.

The door burst open. In came Mom, smiling from ear to ear.

"How was your night, sweetie?" I looked up and smiled weakly. Every muscle in my body ached with pain.

"Fine, Mama." I decided not to tell her about the dream.

Mom went to the closet and pulled out some clothes to help me get dressed. The nurse came in with my little orange and white pills. I swallowed the pills quickly and slowly sank back into my bed, pulling the covers up to my chin.

"Do you want to get dressed, Robin?" Mom asked, holding in her arms a cotton sundress.

"In a minute," I said, knowing it took about twenty minutes for the drugs to take effect.

Jeri bounced through the door, hugged my mom and plopped down on the bed. I winced in pain. She saw my face and knew what my night had been like. She looked at me, and I signaled her not to say anything to my mother. She nodded knowingly. Jeri always understood me.

"Well, girls, what's on the schedule for today?" Mom asked.

"Rehab, rehab, and more rehab," chimed Jeri and me, as if we had rehearsed it.

Jeri slipped some candy bars and a Variety magazine out of her pocket and into my top drawer. I giggled at her sweetness. I felt fortunate to have a friend and a mother like the ones who were standing before me.

Breakfast rolled in on a cart piloted by a hospital worker. He placed the tray in front of me and gave me a look that said, "You had better eat every bite."

I looked down at the Rice Krispies, the bran muffin and the orange juice. After he left the room I reached over, opened my top drawer and snatched out a candy bar.

It was time for my rehabilitation classes. Since Mom and Jeri were there, they helped me into my wheelchair and off we went.

I couldn't shake the memory of the dream. It seemed to be stamped on my mind and kept replaying itself over and over. When we were out of mom's earshot, Jeri whispered in my ear.

"What happened last night?" I quickly told her about the dream.

"That's not the first time you've had that dream," she said.

I nodded and said nothing.

Mom and Jeri watched as I went from one rehab class to another, re-educating my hands, my legs, and my mind to do all the normal functions the accident had stripped away. By the end of the day we were all exhausted.

On the way back to my room Mom asked if she could speak to me alone. Dad would be waiting up in my room, and she said they wanted to talk to me about something important. Always sensitive, Jeri took her cue and went off to the refreshment lounge.

When we arrived back upstairs, Dad was flipping through one of my New Age books on white light healing and positive affirmations.

"Has this positive affirmation stuff helped?" he asked.

"Not really," I said.

"Robin," Mom said, jumping right in, "what are you going to do when you get out of here?" I looked at her. *She wants me to come home so she can take care of me,* I thought to myself.

"Mom, I'm going to be 100 percent better when I get out. I'll be able to take care of myself, plus I'll be near the hospital to continue rehab. The restaurant's worker's compensation insurance is covering all my medical bills, and I'm receiving disability checks and residual checks from all those commercials I did. I'll manage just fine."

"Honey," she said, glancing at my father for support, "we just want what's best for you. Dr. Sellerman said you might need some help after you're released."

"Mom, Jeri said she would stay with me. I'll have a maid, and everything will work out. I have to be at rehab three times a week, and I don't think I should change hospitals."

"Are you sure?" my father said with a look that only a father can give.

"Listen, I love you both very much, but don't worry

about me. I'm going to be fine. I'm going to keep my career. I'm going to dance and act and sing again. I've worked too hard to let this thing beat me."

The time for my release came sooner than I expected. I was finally going home to my apartment in Hollywood. It was late June, 1985. Two months had passed since the accident.

I sat dressed in my wheelchair, waiting patiently for Dr. Sellerman. *When I get home, I will be completely on my own*, I thought as I took a deep breath and fought back a feeling of panic.

Dr. Sellerman entered, followed closely by Jeri. Instinctively I knew they had been talking about me.

"Hey, what took you two so long? I'm ready to break out of this place."

Dr. Sellerman grinned, then said, "I gave Jeri some instructions on your rehab schedule after you get home and what to do in case of an emergency. You know, if a seizure starts and you can't stop it."

"There won't be any emergencies, Doc. I know my stuff."

I saw Dr. Sellerman and Jeri exchange glances, but I didn't care. I was going home. I'd show them all I could do it.

"Well, let's go," Jeri said.

Dr. Sellerman waved good-bye and watched until we turned a corner and were out of sight. Nurses and hospital workers smiled and wished me luck as Jeri wheeled me past. I grinned and tried to contain my excitement. I had hoped that when I left I would be completely normal, but now I didn't care about all that. I was just glad to be leaving!

We were approaching the automatic sliding front door. I

felt like a convict being released from prison. The wide double doors slid open, and I maneuvered my wheelchair through them and out into freedom.

I saw our getaway car parked near the entrance, ready to whisk us away. Jeri helped me into the front seat, put my wheelchair in the back, flipped in a Loverboy tape, and away we flew, music blasting.

"Man, L.A. is great!" I shouted from the window. "I'm free! Let's party." All I could think about was getting some cocaine, some champagne, some liver paté and the latest videos. I was on heavy pain medication around the clock, but I hated the way it made me feel. Maybe with some cocaine and champagne flowing through me I would feel better.

"First thing I have to do is get some money," I said. "Let's go to the bank." I dug in my purse and retrieved my ATM card. "I'm going to spend all this money I've been saving."

Jeri steered the car onto La Cienega Boulevard and passed my theatrical agency.

"Hi, Marvin," I screamed out the window, giggling wildly.

We passed the Screen Actors Guild, and I smiled, knowing I was a full union member. The bank was next. Jeri pulled up to the curb then hopped out of the car. "Give me your card; I'll get the money."

"No, let me get it," I said. I could walk for short distances by now, but not for too long or it could trigger severe spasms. Surely I could make it to the ATM machine. I was eager to try out my wings. Somehow it was very important that I did things on my own.

Jeri helped me out of the car and held my arm as I scooted my way to the machine, taking very small steps. I inserted the card the wrong way, and the machine rejected it. Frowning, I turned it around and inserted it again.

Words flashed up on the miniature screen, asking me to make a selection. My mind went blank. It refused to give me the information I needed to run the ATM machine.

"I've forgotten how to do this," I said, swearing under my breath. "What do I do next?" Tears pooled in my eyes. Jeri stood waiting patiently, not wanting to intrude.

"What do I do next?" I shouted. Panic seized me. I was shocked that I couldn't remember how to do this simple task, and so was my friend.

Suddenly I laughed. I pictured my brain with wires sticking out in all directions, not connected to anything. My brain was like a short-circuiting computer.

"Will you let me do it?" Jeri said. "You were never really any good at ATM machines anyway."

"Sure, but let me watch so I'll know what to do next time."

I watched as she punched in my secret code, which I didn't even remember, and got the money.

She helped me back to the car. Already I was wrestling despair. Reality was closing in on me with frightening clarity.

"I'm going to get completely well," I assured Jeri. "It may just take a little time." Jeri nodded in agreement as she started the engine, but she said nothing. Deep in our hearts we both knew my words might not come true.

My front door was three steps up; the wheel chair couldn't make it. No one had thought of this problem, and I was not strong enough to climb stairs. Finally Jeri had to almost carry me into the apartment and then go back for my wheelchair.

Inside everything looked the same. My cat, Sebastian, jumped on my lap and purred loudly, welcoming me home. Jeri had moved into my apartment over the past few months to take care of him. I hadn't seen Sebastian for a long time, but it looked as if he and Jeri had become best friends.

I smiled at the sight of my familiar things: the modern furniture, the black lacquer tables you could see your reflection in. I loved the multicolored prints, the warmth of the wicker in my kitchen, and the comfort of my own bed. It was all like a little bit of heaven after the sterility of the hospital room. My wheelchair seemed like a foreign object among all these old familiar things. It was a constant reminder that my life was different now.

Jeri waved good-bye as she left to get the cocaine, the champagne, the liver paté and, of course, enough videos to last all night. I hadn't seen any movies for months, and I was hungry to catch up.

As the door shut behind her, I tried to be positive, to look on the bright side. At least I was alive. The accident could have killed me. Yet I couldn't help but be wary of what the future would bring.

"Marilyn, where are you? Why have you left me? Why won't you answer me?" Empty silence hung in the air.

I wheeled myself over to the table and looked down at the pile of unopened mail. After flipping through the first few bills, I came to a letter that caught my interest. It was from Mrs. Langley, the wealthy, influential woman who hosted psychic meetings at her mountain home.

I opened it and read it aloud:

Dear Robin,

We've all missed you very much. We expected you at our last psychic gathering in Northern California. Has something happened? Why haven't you called? We are all worried. Have you closed your mind to us? I can't seem to read your spirit any longer. Please call me.

I sank back in my wheelchair. The words of the letter seemed to hook right into my gut. I fought back a compulsion to go to the phone.

"No, I won't call you. You can't make me call!" I bellowed.

I took a deep breath. After fishing around in my purse for a match, I lit the letter on fire and dropped it in the sink.

Why had I ever gotten involved with those people?

I flipped the phone machine on to check messages, and there was her voice again.

Jeri walked through the door.

"She won't stop calling, Robin. I've erased quite a few of those messages. I didn't want to tell you. I knew it might upset you."

"What do those people want with me?"

"I don't know, but they want you, all right."

"They're convinced you're the missing link to their plan. It's freaky how Marvin fits in like a puzzle piece. It just doesn't strike me as a coincidence the way Steven Baker got your number. The whole thing gives me the chills."

Jeri walked over and erased the voice off the tape.

"Don't answer the phone," she said. "I will. I can deal

with these body snatchers."

"What about Marilyn?" I said. "Is she for me or against me?"

Jeri shook her head and shrugged.

She brought in the bags from the car and filled two crystal glasses with champagne. We toasted my homecoming.

Chapter 14

The Way of Escape

*J*eri came into the room and watched me as I sat in my wheelchair, staring out at the Hollywood sign high up on the hill above me. It had been nearly two months since my release from the hospital. After the first night's reveling, the grim reality of my life had settled over me like a dark cloud, shutting out all else. No more dancing, no more acting, no more being normal. Everything was over. All those years of hard work, of climbing the entertainment ladder, wasted.

"You've lost your smile, Robin," my friend said.

I glanced over at her then turned back to face the open window. I couldn't smile and put on a brave face anymore. All the strength I'd had was gone.

Taking a shower took two hours. I couldn't do anything for myself; I needed constant care. The pain had intensified since I left the hospital because I was forced to do more, move more. Seizures overwhelmed me any time I exerted myself in any way. I had become a prisoner in my own body. I wanted out.

"Come on, let's get going," Jeri said, her voice interrupting my thoughts. "You don't want to be late for your appointment."

After struggling into the car from my wheelchair, I leaned back and closed my eyes, not wanting to look out the window as we drove to the hospital. I had been seen by a host of doctors and therapists since the accident, and most of them were waiting for me as I wheeled into the hospital boardroom. I pulled myself up to the table, remembering the conversation with Christy just before she went home.

Thick file folders lay on the shiny oval table in front of each doctor. Scattered here and there were half empty cups of coffee, growing colder by the minute.

Dr. Sellerman cleared his throat to begin the meeting. He seemed to be the spokesperson for the group.

"We have been re-evaluating your case, Robin, and we've come to some conclusions." I braced myself for the inevitable.

"We feel that we have done all that can be accomplished through this facility." The words hung heavy in the air.

"Are you going to transfer me somewhere else?" I stammered.

"Robin," said Dr. Sellerman, "we feel that your recovery has come as far as it is going to come. We are closing your case except for weekly sessions with Dr. Harris."

Dr. Harris was a psychiatrist who had the look of an escaped mental ward patient. I looked over at him, and he smiled a "cerebral egghead" smile at me. "Of course, there will still be monthly visits with me," Dr. Sellerman added.

"Thank you very much. Thank you all very much," I said as I turned and wheeled myself through the doors and down the long hallway to the phone.

"Come and get me, Jeri," I said in a monotone. "I finished early today."

I hung up the phone and broke into sobs.

Jeri drove me home in silence. Tears slipped down my cheeks onto my lap. All life seemed to be still and silent.

"Jeri, I want you to leave," I said softly, choking back a lump in my throat. "You've given me months of your time, but this project is finished. I want you to get on with your life. I won't need you to drive me to the hospital any longer, and I can't allow you to throw your life away." She didn't even look at me. She just kept driving. I stared out the window as if it were the bars of a cage.

"Dr. Sellerman suggested that I take you to see Dr. Harris. Did he tell you that?" she said finally.

"Do you mean a shrink? You mean I should go just to hear him tell me my life has consisted of a series of abusive relationships resulting from deep insecurity? No thank you."

Tense silence filled the car.

"Robin, you really should think about it." She pulled into the driveway of my apartment. I looked up and saw the Hollywood sign on the hill.

"What a joke," I hissed. "It should say Hellwood, home of broken dreams and discarded dreamers."

Jeri helped me into the house and went into the kitchen to make some coffee. I shuffled in behind her, then supported myself on the counter.

"Jeri, you have got to leave. I don't want you here anymore." I was getting angry. She didn't seem to be paying any attention to me. I said it again, this time even louder and stressing every syllable.

"You have got to leave. I want to be alone. You're a dancer; you're an actress; you have a life. Please leave me alone! Got it?"

I became hysterical, and a seizure hit. My hands gripped the countertop for support. Jeri ran over to me and tried to help me to my bed. I fought her off and plopped down in my wheelchair.

"No!" I screamed out in rage. "Just get out of here and leave me alone!"

She handed me two pills and a glass of water. I slapped them out of her hands, spilling the water everywhere.

"I don't want your help. Don't you understand? Get out of here."

Jeri calmly bent down to wipe up the water, then finally spoke.

"All right, Robin, I'll leave. I'll go to my mom's and call you later," she said evenly, trying to control her temper. She put the pills on the kitchen table.

"Take your things with you," I shrieked hysterically "I don't want you to ever come back."

I watched, still gripped by the seizure, as she packed a small bag and left the apartment. After the door closed behind her, I gulped down the two pills then wheeled myself over to the phone machine and flipped it on. I needed some peace and quiet. Propelling my wheelchair down the dim hallway, I maneuvered myself into bed and pulled the covers up over my face. Somehow I managed to fall asleep.

Light streamed through the mini-blinds in my bedroom, announcing the start of another day. I lay in bed and stared vacantly at the ceiling. It was late August.

Ring...Ring...Ring. The phone machine picked up the call. I listened as my perky voice—the voice that belonged to the old Robin—answered, "I can't come to the phone right now, but if you leave your name and number, I'll be sure and get back with you."

"Baby, it's Mom. Are you there? Ok, I'm home. You must be at rehab. Call me later. I love you." The phone machine cut off.

I pulled myself out of bed and made my way to the kitchen, bracing on the furniture. I opened the cabinet and saw freshly renewed prescriptions of pain pills. As I stared at the bottles of yellow and red pills, the thought hit me.

"That's it," I said out loud. "I'll take an overdose of pills."

Time seemed to stand still. I could see the news story before my eyes:

DANCER-ACTRESS FOUND DEAD IN HOLLYWOOD APARTMENT

LOS ANGELES—Police discovered the body of a woman in a Hollywood apartment Friday, the apparent victim of a suicide. The deceased, 28-year-old Robin Harry, suffered a debilitating accident four months ago that sent her career as a successful dancer-actress on the skids. An empty bottle of barbiturates was found beside the body. Members of the deceased's family have requested an autopsy to rule out suspicion of foul play....

The loud ringing of the telephone interrupted my thoughts. I waited until the phone machine clicked on.

"Hey, Robin, are you there?" a familiar voice said. "Do

you want to go to church tonight? I thought maybe you could use some company. If you do, give me a call."

The caller hung up. It was Prescott, the bass player for Brian's rock band. Ever since he had become "born again," as he called it, he hadn't been the same. This was the third or fourth time he had invited me to church.

I looked again at the bottle of pills. I wanted to do it—there was no other way out—but fear churned in my stomach. It wouldn't hurt to prolong the inevitable a little longer. *Maybe I'll just go to church with Prescott and then do it when I get back.*

I reached for the phone and dialed Prescott's number.

Chapter 15

Meeting God

J had three hours before Prescott would arrive to pick me up. Given my physical limitations, I decided to shower and start dressing right away. It would take that long. As I shuffled to the bathroom, the telephone rang. As usual, I let the answering machine screen the call for me.

"Robin, please pick up the phone," Jeri's voice pleaded. "This isn't fair. Are you all right?"

She hung up.

The phone rang again. This time it was Prescott.

"Hey, Robin, pick up," I heard him say.

"Hello," I said as I picked up the receiver. "What's up?"

"Robin, thank God I caught you. My car broke down on the freeway. I'm going to have the tow truck driver drop me by the church. Could you call someone to give you a ride?"

This is my way out, I thought.

"Listen, maybe it isn't such a good idea for me to come anyway," I said.

"No, Robin, you've just got to come!" he said. There was an urgency in his voice.

"Ok, calm down," I said. "I'll try."

After showering, I got dressed then looked for my car keys.

"I shouldn't be trying this," I mumbled. I hadn't driven since the day of the accident. My driver's license was no longer current, and I had taken enough pain pills to kill myself and anyone else I might crash into.

Leaving the wheelchair just inside the front door, I slowly made my way down the three steps and over to the driveway. By my calculations, I had approximately forty minutes out of the wheelchair before a seizure would hit. I was taking a chance on having a seizure in public, but somehow it didn't seem to matter. Somehow it seemed natural for me to go.

"I hope this won't take long," I said out loud as I edged carefully into my Porsche. "Then I'll come back home, swallow every pill I can find, lie down and just go to sleep forever."

It sounded so easy, but I was actually scared to death. I was scared to go through with it, but also scared to go on living. *I'm not good for anything anymore. This way I won't be a burden to anybody—not Jeri, not my parents, nobody. I'm just tired. Tired of being in pain all the time.*

Hollywood Presbyterian happened to be just three blocks down the hill from my apartment. I wouldn't have to drive far. Somehow I maneuvered the car safely down the hill. It seemed easy to handle, a lot easier than I had expected. There was no traffic, which is a miracle for any street in L.A.

I made it to the church. As I pulled into the parking lot, I noticed a young man with jet black hair who was dressed in a suit standing in front of the small chapel where the service was to be held. He had gentle eyes, but those eyes watched me keenly as I brought my Porsche to a safe landing. Later I found out the young man's name was Christian Harfouche. An interim pastor at a local church, he and another guest preacher would be conducting the Friday night chapel service, which was titled "Life in the Spirit."

I struggled out of my car and immediately felt the presence of an unseen power all around me. I had always been sensitive to spiritual feelings and spiritual presences, but this was different. My heart pounded as I walked toward the chapel. I saw the young man enter by a side door.

By the time I reached the chapel doors, my stomach was doing flip-flops. I knew something extraordinary was about to take place. As I opened the double doors and stepped inside, a warm, tingly sensation shot through me, sending heat into every fiber of my being.

The service was already in progress. I slipped into one of the velvet-covered pews in the back. As I listened to the thirty or so people gathered there sing softly, tears trickled down my cheeks. I quickly brushed them away, hoping no one would notice. The people's voices sounded like angels singing. It was beautiful.

I looked up at the A-framed oak ceiling, the stained-glass windows, and inhaled the rich, wood-scented air, tinged slightly with the smell of sulfur from the candles. It had been a long time since I had been in a church. I felt warm and safe here.

What is this place? I wondered. *It's just a plain, ordinary church, but where is this power coming from?*

"Hi, Robin," a voice said. I turned to look as Prescott scooted in beside me. "Are you all right? Are you in pain?"

I nodded, lying, because pain made a good excuse for the tears. I didn't understand what was happening to me, and I couldn't talk about it right then.

I glanced around at the people in the chapel. Most of them were humble, modest people, not flashy Hollywood types like me. There was a woman up front playing a few chords on a guitar. I saw the young man I had seen outside standing on the platform.

As the people continued to sing, Prescott included, some of them lifted their hands high, their faces turned upward. They sang beautiful songs of love to God, then they all began to sing in a strange language I didn't understand. As they sang, I was touched by the beauty of their voices blending together. Fresh tears poured down my cheeks.

And then a realization hit me.

"I'm not in pain," I said to Prescott, my eyes wide with disbelief. He just looked at me and smiled and continued to sing.

When the singing was over, a man walked to the front and began to speak. As he preached, his words pricked my heart. He told the simple story of how Jesus came and died on the cross of Calvary, how He gave His life for me so that I wouldn't have to spend eternity apart from Him: an eternity in hell. He said that Jesus is the only way to God and that all other ways are forged from lies and deception.

Something leaped inside me. I knew that for the first time in my life I was hearing the truth. Not just a truth, but *the* Truth. At that moment I realized that Jesus Christ was God. All those years of seeking, all those hours of studying and training for the New Age, all those tormented nights when sleep eluded me all seemed insignificant now that I saw Jesus, as it were, face to face. I closed my eyes, whispering a prayer.

Suddenly Marilyn's image intruded into my mind. Then I watched in horror as a deceiving facade peeled away. Gone was the svelte feminine form, the platinum hair, the pretty, pouting face. In their place was a hideous black creature with sunken features and twisted, claw-like hands. Its bulging yellow eyes glowed with evil. Then I knew: Marilyn was an evil spirit that had lied to me and wanted me to deceive others. I never should have listened to her—or Marvin, or Mrs. Langley.

I opened my eyes to avoid the horrible image. At the same instant I heard a scream inside my head.

"You wouldn't go all the way! You could have had it all. I'm the one who wanted you dead. You knew too much! You knew all about the plan!" the croaking voice said.

I heard one last scream, a shriek of defeat, then silence. The spirit's grip on me was gone.

The preacher stopped speaking and asked those six who wanted to accept Jesus to come forward. There was no holding back now.

"I need God," I whispered as I pulled myself toward the aisle to make my way up front. "The real God."

"You are being healed," I heard the man say as I fell backward, hit by some unseen power. But the man had not even touched me. Someone caught me and lowered me gently to the floor.

As I lay there, wrapped in the same intense heat I had felt when I came through the door, I began to shake. Sobs racked my body. I couldn't control myself. Then I felt someone's arms go around me.

This is not a seizure, I thought as my body trembled. Something incredible was happening. After forty-five minutes of crying, I looked up into the face of the woman who was holding me.

"I was all wrong," I choked out. "Jesus is God, the real God. He's the only way."

"I know, sweetheart," she smiled. "You're all right. That's just the power of God all over you. That's Jesus."

She helped me to my feet. As I stood, I was astonished to discover that all of the muscles in my body worked. They were supple, not clenched into rock-hard knots. For the first time in months I could turn my neck from side to side. My back could move, my waist could move and my legs felt limber and strong again, just like a dancer's ought to. Best of all, I could walk normally, and the constant pain I had lived with for four months was gone.

The tiny chapel was filled with commotion as people left the service. No one seemed to realize what had just happened to me. I didn't really know myself. I looked around but couldn't find Prescott. Dumbfounded, I sat down on the front pew to sort things out. I saw two black shoes approaching.

I raised my head and looked into the face of the young man I had seen earlier at the front of the church. "Are you all right?" he asked

Our eyes connected.

"I'm fine, I guess," I said, "How are you?"

He smiled.

There was something gentle yet very strong about this man, something I had never seen before. We started to talk a little more.

"I'm a preacher," he said in answer to one of my questions, his eyes shining with pride.

"I'm a dancer," I said. At the sound of my own words, I started to weep. *I really am a dancer*, I realized. *I'm healed.*

"Are you a Christian?" he asked. I looked at him, then broke into a huge smile.

"Yes. Yes, I am."

Chapter 16

A New Life

J pulled into my driveway, turned off the ignition and just sat there for a minute, hands gripping the steering wheel as I let the events of the past two hours sink in. It was all too unbelievable, yet here I was, living proof that it had happened. That intense heat still permeated my body. Wiping my brow, I finally picked up my purse and got out.

"Now here comes the real test," I said as I approached the steps to my front door. Without pausing to think, I leaped up to the second step then sprang onto the small landing, laughing in simple delight.

I fumbled in my purse for the key to my apartment, then opened the door, not prepared for what hit me.

This is God, I heard in my spirit, and the words seemed as vivid as an audible voice. *You have been healed.*

This voice was different from the others that used to torment me. It didn't fill me with dread but rather an over-whelming sense of peace and joy. And I *had* been healed.

There sat my wheelchair, its metal spokes gleaming in the dark. It looked like the discarded implement it had become. I walked past the wheelchair straight into my bedroom.

"Where is all this heat coming from?" I said, changing my dress for a set of shorts and a T-shirt with the neck cut out.

Still burning up, I went into the bathroom and leaned over the sink to wash my face with cold water. I groped for a hand towel, patted my face dry and opened my eyes. As I gazed in the mirror, I saw the eyes of Jesus looking out from my face.

I stood transfixed for a moment, then said softly, "I was going to kill myself tonight, Jesus. You took me from death to life. You healed me. Anything You tell me to do, I'll do. Even if it means breaking up with Brian. Just say the word. My life doesn't belong to me anymore. It's Yours, God, all of it."

As I stood there, gazing in the mirror, God began to speak to my heart, giving me instructions. Again speaking in an inner voice, He told me to take all the drugs in my apartment and throw them in the dumpster outside. Next He told me to throw out all the occult paraphernalia I had accumulated over the years: my crystals, my books, my tarot cards, my New Age tapes, everything. When I cleaned out my bookshelf, all that remained was a little paperback Bible I had picked up at a drugstore months earlier.

My chores accomplished, I sat down on the living room sofa. It had been four hours since my last dose of Percodan. My system craved another boost. I shifted nervously, wondering what to do next. I had heard about what happens to people when they go cold turkey off drugs.

"Jesus, help me," I whispered.

You will go through two days of drug withdrawals, the inner voice said. *On Monday you will be well. Do not worry because I will be with you all the time.*

The next forty-eight hours were the most difficult of my life. I spent most of those hours curled up on the bathroom floor in a cold sweat, vomiting every so often. But, true to His word, Jesus was there with me, speaking gently to my heart and filling my mind with Scripture.

Gradually the vomiting turned to dry heaves, and finally nothing at all. As the sun sent the gray light of dawn through my window that Monday morning, I lay down on my bed and slept like a baby. All the withdrawal symptoms were gone.

The days passed quickly. I found myself looking forward to Friday night. Christian had invited me to come back to the chapel and tell the people what God had done for me. On Wednesday evening Brian popped by to see me. When I opened the door to his knock, I twirled around to show him my newfound agility, giggling like a little girl.

"How do I look?" I said, beaming. Gone were the haggard lines of depression. And I had taken the time to do my hair and apply makeup that day.

"You...you look great," he stammered, his mouth agape. "You look like yourself again. What happened?"

"Oh, Brian, you won't believe it!" I said excitedly as I pulled him through the door and steered him to my couch. "There, sit down. Just listen to this. It's incredible." And off I went on a wild soliloquy recounting the miracles of the past week: my release from Marilyn, my physical healing, my withdrawal from barbiturates and, most of all, my new relationship with Jesus Christ.

Brian was quiet, not excited as I had expected.

"Robin, I'm really happy for you, don't get me wrong. I just don't want to see these people use you."

"No, Brian, you don't understand. These are just plain folks. They're not like Mrs. Langley's crowd. Don't worry about me. This time it's really God."

He fidgeted with his car keys and looked down at his lap. "So what does this mean as far as you and I are concerned?"

Now I was silent. Over the past few days I had been wrestling with the persistent thought that I should break up with Brian, now that my life had changed.

"I don't know, Brian," I said finally "Let's just take it one step at a time. So much has happened to me this week. Oh, did I tell you the young preacher who was there wants me to come back this Friday night and tell everyone what happened?"

Brian's brow creased.

"Who is this guy?"

"Oh, don't be silly," I laughed. "He's just some preacher. You don't need to worry. He's square."

"Maybe I better go with you," he said, his face still lined with concern. "Oh, wait a minute. I can't. I've gotta work Friday night. Listen, baby, I just stopped by to say hello. I'm on my way to the recording studio. I've gotta run."

I walked him to the door.

"You'll call me and let me know how it goes on Friday?" he asked.

"Of course I will," I said, then kissed him lightly on the lips. I stood on the doorstep and watched as this handsome man who had become such an important part of my life drove away in his bright red sports car. As he disappeared over the crest of the hill, I wrapped my arms around myself.

"Good-bye, Brian," I said quietly, and turned to go back inside.

The next morning I drove myself to Dr. Sellerman's office for my monthly checkup. I couldn't help grinning at the thought of what his reaction would be. At the same time I was nervous about how to tell him.

"Hi, Grace," I said to the nurse as I walked in the door, smiling broadly.

"Wow, you look terrific!" she answered. "Go on in. He'll be with you in a minute." I stepped into the examination room and hopped onto the table, deciding not to put on the gown.

"Jesus, give me the right words," I prayed under my breath.

At that moment Dr. Sellerman opened the door, walked right up to me and said, "What happened to you?"

Before I could answer he blurted out, "Are you off the drugs?"

"Yes."

"What?" It was almost a shriek, "Tell me what happened."

"'Do you want to sit down?" I laughed. "It's a long story."

Dr. Sellerman took a seat, placed his clipboard on his lap and stared at me, waiting patiently.

"All right," I said, taking a deep breath. "This is going to sound strange, but I went to church last Friday night, and some people prayed for me. Heat came on me like nothing I've ever felt before, and it's been on me for seven days. When I left the church, I wasn't in pain anymore and all my muscles worked normally. I no longer wanted to take the drugs so I threw them all out and—"

"Robin," he interrupted, "don't you realize you could have hurt yourself by withdrawing cold turkey like that? If you really wanted off them that badly, why didn't you tell me? I could've reduced the dosages gradually. You're lucky you didn't have heart failure."

"But, Dr. Sellerman, watch this," I said. I jumped off the table and demonstrated my flexibility, touching my toes, twisting my trunk and so forth.

"Look, just put the gown on," he said, standing to leave. "I still want to examine you." He re-entered the room a few minutes later and gave me a thorough examination.

"I don't believe it," he said as he prodded the muscles along my spine. "The spasms in your muscles are all gone. Everywhere."

"I know they are," I said, smiling.

He stepped back and eyed me with the look of one who doesn't quite believe what he is seeing.

"I don't know what to say. This *must* be God," he said. "But I want to see you again next week."

He picked up his clipboard and left the room. Friday night came and with it my debut before a crowd of eager Christians. I was nervous as I walked to the platform to give my *testimony*, as they called it.

I glanced at the front pew. There sat Christian, his face all smiles. *Oh, dear God, please don't let this guy fall for me. He's not my type.*

I looked back at the audience to collect my thoughts. Not exactly sure where to start, I plunged in and told the whole story from my occult experiences to my healing and deliverance. As I talked, tears came to my eyes, and I was surprised to see everyone in the chapel grow misty-eyed as well.

"All I know is this," I said finally, coming to a close. "Jesus Christ is God, and He healed me. I have no more pain and no more need for drugs." The people broke into spontaneous applause, then stood to their feet and raised their hands, talking to God in that strange language I'd heard the week before.

Not sure what to do, I stepped off the platform and walked back to my seat. Someone started playing the piano, and the woman with the guitar picked up the chords. I clapped my hands and joined in the lively singing, following along with the words printed on the overhead projector. After about thirty minutes of singing, the service was dismissed. People crowded around me, each one eager to meet me and give me a hug. I saw Christian hanging back near the platform, talking to this and that person and shaking hands. But every so often he glanced in my direction. After the crowd around me had dispersed, I headed for the door.

"Wait," I heard a voice say.

I knew without looking who it was.

"Yes?" I said, turning to face Christian. "How'd I do?"

He smiled.

"You were great. Praise the Lord." We stood there, caught in an awkward silence.

"Listen," he added, "we have a Bible study at my house every Tuesday night. Would you like to come next week?"

"Sure, I'll come," I said, grinning at his nervousness. "Call me later and give me directions."

I jotted down my phone number, waved good-bye and walked out to my car.

The Bible study was located in a small town called La Puente.

"La who?" I had said when Christian called to give me directions. "I've never heard of it."

As it turned out, La Puente was only about twenty minutes south of Los Angeles. Several times on the trip down I had to pull off the road and squint at the fine print on the map to make sure I was following the correct routes. My shiny black Porsche brought stares as it snaked in and out of the meager La Puente traffic. This was certainly no Tinsel Town. Dark haired teenagers clustered on nearly every street corner; I eyed them warily, hoping none of them was in the market for hubcaps.

At last I brought my Porsche to a stop in front of a house that matched the address Christian had given me. The windows of all the houses I could see were covered with burglar bars, except for his house. A handful of other cars were parked in the driveway and along the curb.

Fifteen minutes late, I slipped in the front door. The small group gathered there had just formed a circle and were about to pray.

"I knew you would come tonight," a man said, leaving the circle to grasp my hand. I recognized him as the man who had been preaching the night I was healed.

"When I was praying earlier this evening, the Lord showed me He was going to fill you with the Holy Spirit..."

Before he even got the word "Spirit" out, I was knocked flat on the floor by the same unseen power I had felt the night I was healed. Oddly enough, the fall did not hurt. I felt as though I had floated to the terrazzo floor. Suddenly I heard the sound of my own voice. But the words coming from my mouth were not in English. I was speaking in the same strange language I had heard the others use before.

Hands reached out to pull me to my feet. Instinctively I turned to Christian for explanation.

"What was that?" I said, my eyes wide.

"That was the baptism of the Holy Spirit," he answered gently.

I didn't know what to say. Everything had been happening too fast in the past eleven days, as if I were on a whirlwind tour with God.

After the Bible study, Christian walked me out to my car. I was worried that he was getting too interested, but I didn't want to seem unfriendly. I was relieved to see all four hubcaps intact.

"Well, I'll see you later," I said briskly as I unlocked the car door. He stood there, not taking the hint.

"Robin, I'm going to be in Hollywood tomorrow. Would you mind if Julie and I stopped by to see you late afternoon?"

I thought for a moment. He was playing it safe, bringing along another girl—the one who always played the guitar. But what did it matter to me? I would just as soon have it that way.

"Sure, that'd be great. My schedule isn't exactly hectic these days," I added with a grin.

"Good. I'll see you then," he said, looking at me intently.

As I drove out of La Puente and headed back toward Hollywood, I smiled to myself. It had been a long time since I had come across a man who got shy in the presence of a pretty woman. It was kind of sweet—even if that man was just a preacher from La Puente.

Chapter 17

A Tender Miracle

After I arrived home from the Bible study that night, I heard one clear instruction from the inner voice that I knew was God: You must cut off all ties with your past, even your relationships with Brian and Jeri. Although I sensed Brian had seen it coming, the telephone call to him was difficult. Jeri was another matter. Our parting had been so heated that I shrank from calling her at all, afraid that any words I offered would sound hollow after my treatment of her. In the end I didn't contact her at all, but prayed that God would somehow reconcile us to each other when the time was right.

It was more like early evening when Christian and Julie finally rang my doorbell the next day. For some reason I had butterflies in my stomach.

As I opened the door for my new friends, I tried to disguise my nervousness. "Hi, guys, come on in," I said brightly.

They took a seat in the living room, and I offered them iced cappuccino. As we drank the cool liquid, I learned more about Christian's background. He had earned a black belt in karate, but when the Lord called him to preach, he said that martial arts and everything else in his life were no longer important to him. He talked on about God, his eyes shining. I felt the Holy Spirit's presence in the room.

"Sometimes the Word of God is like a burning fire in my head," he said, leaning forward. "Does that make any sense? I feel like the apostle Paul; I can't help but preach the gospel." There was an intensity in this man that I had never encountered before. I had always been attracted to strong personalities, people who knew where they were going. But this man was different. He had no obsessive drive to reach the top, no reckless abandon to pursue his goals. Instead, there seemed a quiet steadiness about him, a sense of purpose, a sense of destiny.

As the hours passed, what had been a gentle summer breeze churned into a thunderstorm. The dark sky rumbled overhead and the palm fronds outside my window rattled in the fury of the wind. We moved to the balcony to watch the storm.

"Robin, how are you doing?" Christian asked.

"I'm fine."

"No, I mean really," he pressed. "You've come through quite a radical change in your life from heavy involvement in the New Age movement to Christianity. How have you been doing spiritually?"

"Well," I stammered, "I have had several nightmares lately, and I've been tormented with thoughts of demons. You know, the way Marilyn really looked, and all."

"I see," Christian said. He was quiet for a moment. "I think there are a few things we need to pray about."

We joined hands, and Christian prayed that God would be my Comforter and protect me from demonic attack. He rebuked any evil spirits that were trying to torment me. Then he placed his hands on my head and prophesied over me, saying that God had a calling on my life and that He wanted to use me.

"All of the spiritual sensitivity you possess, God will turn around and use for His glory to bless many people," he said. Goosebumps broke out on my arms as I remembered my prayer as a little girl, lying in the alfalfa field: *When I grow up, I want to help people to feel.*

Christian finished by praying a blessing on my life. He opened his eyes and smiled at me. I smiled back. Julie glanced back and forth at the two of us.

Suddenly I felt compelled to return the favor. Placing my hands on Christian's head, I prophesied over him the way I had been trained to do as a New Ager.

"Christian," I said, "I see you in a car. You're in a bad part of town, and as you pull up to a stop sign, a guy who also knows karate comes up to your car and threatens you. You get out of the car and fight him. You are victorious. You kill him."

Christian looked at me, took my hands off his head and backed away a few steps.

"Robin," he said gently, "maybe you should sit down. There's something we need to talk about."

I took a seat and waited for him to speak.

"You remember how when you were into the New Age you used to prophesy by the power of your spirit guide?" he asked.

As soon as his words were out I sensed I had done

wrong. Tears sprang to my eyes, and I nodded, not saying anything.

"Well, there are two realms in the spirit. There's the realm of the Holy Spirit, which is the realm of God, and there's the psychic realm, which is the realm of Satan. Because of your involvement in the psychic realm, we need to pray the prayer of deliverance so that those fake gifts will no longer operate in you."

"But how will I know it's really God and not what I used to do?" I asked.

"After we pray Jesus will shut that door. As you grow in the Lord and learn the Word, the Bible, you will always be able to discern between the two. Your spirit will know."

"I'm so sorry," I said, covering my face. "I don't want to do anything that's not of God anymore." Tears streamed down my cheeks, and I felt the powerful presence of the Holy Spirit.

"That's alright. You're still just a baby Christian," Christian said, grinning. "God knows your heart. Now stand up. I'm going to pray for you." I stood to my feet. The storm had subsided, leaving in its wake a cool, gentle breeze.

Christian placed his hands on my head and prayed again, this time in a stern, authoritative voice. He commanded the spirits of the occult to leave. I felt something lurch inside me.

At that instant the telephone rang. I screamed, sensing the sudden presence of evil. Christian grabbed me and held me tight. I couldn't stop shaking. The phone machine clicked on, and the three of us stood silently as Brian's voice came on the line.

"Robin, are you there? Are you there? If you are, please

pick up. I need to talk to you."

I knew I didn't dare pick up the telephone.

Somehow it seemed connected with the presence of evil that had filled the room. I had broken up with Brian. He, and my past, had no part in me now.

As we stood there, Christian's arms still around me, I was flooded with an overwhelming sense of love for this man. All traces of evil fled, and the balcony became a holy place, a private sanctuary for God, Christian, and me. Even Julie was gone; sensing the moment, she had excused herself to the restroom.

I cradled my head on Christian's shoulder. He remained silent and kept holding me until I stopped trembling. I felt protected in his arms and didn't want to leave. This was a love I'd never experienced before; our very hearts seemed joined as one.

Suddenly that inner voice I recognized as God said, "This is the man you are going to marry." The words were so clear that I could not mistake them.

I backed away and looked up at Christian, searching his eyes. Had he heard the voice too? He gazed back at me a moment.

"I'd better go," he said. He and Julie left.

I tried to pretend everything was the same as I readied myself for bed that night. But that incredible feeling of love and God's surprising words to me kept replaying in my mind. I snuggled under my blanket and fell into a deep, peaceful sleep.

Christian called me the next morning from his church office. We talked for three hours. Toward the end of the conversation, I drummed up the courage to say what had been on my mind all morning.

"Last night, when you hugged me, was that you or was that God?" I said.

"What do you mean?" came his reply.

"Well, when you hugged me, I felt love like I've never known before. I need to know: was that love from you or God?"

Christian cleared his throat.

"It was the Lord," he said. But I was not convinced.

An awkward silence followed, then Christian mentioned that he and some friends were going to Disneyland that coming Saturday.

"Can I come too?" I blurted out. "Oh, I'm sorry, that sounded rude. Never mind. It's just that I don't have anyone to hang out with anymore. I don't want to be around my old friends anymore; you know, the party life-style and everything."

"No, no, it's all right," he laughed. "I'd love for you to come. We'll pick you up at 7:30."

Saturday morning I woke with a feeling of anticipation. After gulping down a doughnut and a cup of coffee, I pulled on a pair of khaki shorts and a cotton blouse, then sat on the balcony and waited for Christian. The September sun was warm, but a hint of coming autumn freshened the air. I wished I were in Napa Valley right then, munching one of Grandma's apples, plucked right from the tree....

A honk brought me back to the present. There was Christian, stepping out of the car and coming up the side-walk. I waved and went to meet him at the door.

The friends he had mentioned turned out to be another couple, Rick and Karen. Christian and I sat in the back seat and talked easily the whole way to Disneyland. Once inside the park, the four of us went from one ride to another, talking and laughing. I was glad I had come.

"Hey, guys, come on," Rick said, "there's the Pirates of the Caribbean."

The rest of us groaned in unison as we looked at the long line that wound back and forth outside the entrance to the ride. But we decided to wait anyway. Everything in the park was getting crowded. As we inched closer to the entrance, a Disney employee opened the barricade, looked right at Christian and me and said, "How would you like to get on the ride right now? I've got room for two."

"We'll take it," Christian said, grabbing my hand.

As we hurried toward the entrance he called back over his shoulder, "Rick, we'll catch up with you later."

Once inside the dimly lit tunnel, we found ourselves in yet another line leading to the little boats that would carry us through the ride. Christian still held my hand. It felt very natural. Because of the throng of other tourists around us, we were forced to stand very close to each other.

"Robin, there's something I need to tell you," he said, looking deep into my eyes.

I nodded, waiting.

"Something's been going around in my spirit, and I can't deny it any longer," he said. "I love you."

"What?"

"I love you," he repeated.

"You mean like a sister or a friend or something?"

"Not exactly."

I looked down for a moment.

"Christian," I said at last, "remember when you held me

the other night and I later asked you whether that was you or God, and you said it was God?"

"Yes."

"Well, when you were holding me, I thought I heard God tell me that you and I were supposed to be..."

"Yes, go on," he said.

"Well, married. But that's incredible," I added hurriedly, "because we don't really even know each other."

I watched his face, waiting for a reaction. I needed to know it was actually God's voice I had heard that night.

After a long pause Christian answered, his eyes shining.

"Robin, that night you came to my house for the Bible study and got filled with the Holy Spirit, the Lord told me the same thing. He told me you were going to be my wife."

As we stood there together, pressed in from all sides in the midst of the musty tunnel, I knew that God had worked yet another miracle: He had taken two unlikely strangers and knitted their hearts as one.

"So, am I your type?" I teased, wanting to keep things light.

Christian pretended to be deep in thought for a minute.

"Well, I know my mother was praying for a nice pastor's daughter who plays the piano." We laughed together. Suddenly we found ourselves at the front of the line, and there was our little boat, waiting to carry us through the unknown waters ahead.

"You know," I said as we settled into the wobbly craft, "in my craziest dreams I never imagined I'd end up marrying a preacher."

Back at my apartment, I began to think about the past two weeks. Since my healing, my body had returned to complete normalcy in every way. Only one question remained: Could I still dance?

The day had dawned cool and brisk. I stepped out onto the balcony and gazed up at the Hollywood sign. Funny. The sight of that word emblazoned across the hillside no longer evoked within me the obsession to achieve. Somehow it didn't even matter whether Hollywood ever learned my name or not. And now I was going to marry a preacher.

The day was wasting. I snapped out of my reverie and walked deliberately over to the phone. I knew what I had to do. After making a call, I pulled on my leotards, picked up my purse and went outside to my car.

I drove to the studio in West Hollywood where I had taught so many dance classes over the past several years. Wearing sunglasses to remain incognito, I hurried to the vacant second-story dance room that I had reserved for a couple of hours.

The room brought back a flood of memories. Its smooth hardwood floor, the mirror that extended across one entire wall, the ballet barre stretched across the wall opposite. I locked the door behind me and walked to the middle of the dance floor. High up on the wall to my left was a single window.

"Ok God, this is it," I said.

I had no music, only the music inside my soul.

Beginning with simple warm-up stretches, I gradually increased the intensity of the exercises until I knew I was ready to dance, if dance I still could.

Holding my breath, I started to move in soft, balletic steps. I pirouetted once, then twice, then a third time. Joy bubbled up inside me, and I was all over the room, dancing and leaping and twirling and kicking as high as my head. I laughed in sheer delight as I moved about the room. I danced as I had never danced before. It was an expression of thanks, of utter praise, to God and God alone.

Overcome, I suddenly stopped and sank to the floor in tears. The gentle presence of the Holy Spirit hovered around me.

"Father...Father," I repeated over and over. It was all I could say.

But God knew my heart, just as Christian had told me. God knew the questions that had been tumbling through my head during the past two weeks. What would I do with my life now? I couldn't go back to the way things were before.

How was Christian going to fit into my life? He was a preacher; I, a dancer—yes, yes, I was a dancer again! One thing I did know: Everything in my life would have to change.

As I sat there on my knees, head bowed in humility and speechless gratitude, the Lord spoke to my spirit.

"I am the director of your life now," He said in a still, small voice. "And I will write the script."

As if in confirmation of those words, the hazy light filtering through the window broke into a brilliant ray, forming a natural spotlight from the heavens. I looked up at the window to find its source. The sun, fettered by a dark cloud, had broken free from its chains.

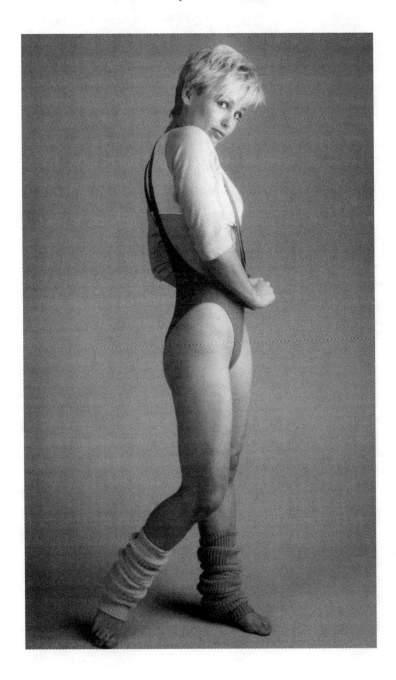

*Robin Harfouche today
with her husband Christian
and their children John and Christie*

would like to pray for you. If possible, please include a photo of yourself
along with your prayer request. The information you share with me is
strictly confidential.

Robin, please pray for me. I need healing for:

- Molestation
- Rape
- Abuse; sexual, physical or verbal
- Sexual perversion
- Depression
- Abusive divorce
- Anorexia
- Bulimia
- Drug addiction, including prescription drugs
- Alcoholism
- Demonic visions or experiences
- Nightmares
- Suicide attempts or thoughts
- Illness or disease of any kind in my physical body
- Fear/Phobias
- Other _____
- I want to know Jesus Christ personally and experience His love.
- I want to be filled with His Spirit.

would like to write back to you. Please let me know your
mailing address.

Name _____

Address _____

City _____ State _____

_____ Country _____

Phone (_____)_____

Email _____

From Hollywood to Heaven

Complete the information below to receive additional copies of the book *From Hollywood to Heaven.*

❏ Please send me _____copies at $12.95 each $_____

  plus shipping and handling at $1.50 each $_____

  Total $_____

(Please print)

Name _____

Address _____

City_____ State_____ Zip_____

Phone (_____)_____ Email_____

Enclosed is   ❏ Check   ❏ Money order

in the amount of $_____

(Please make checks or money orders payable to *REACH*)

Please place my purchase on

❏ Visa   ❏ Mastercard   ❏ American Express

In the amount of $_____

Card number_____ Exp. Date_____

_____
Signature as on card